# The Teacher's Principal

## Also by Jen Schwanke

*You're the Principal! Now What? Strategies and Solutions for New School Leaders*

*The Principal Reboot: 8 Ways to Revitalize Your School Leadership*

# The
# Teacher's
# Principal

**How School
Leaders
Can Support
and Motivate
Their Teachers**

**JEN SCHWANKE**

ascd | Arlington, Virginia USA

2800 Shirlington Road, Suite 1001 • Arlington, VA 22206 USA
Phone: 800-933-2723 or 703-578-9600 • Fax: 703-575-5400
Website: www.ascd.org • Email: member@ascd.org
Author guidelines: www.ascd.org/write

Penny Reinart, *Chief Impact Officer;* Genny Ostertag, *Managing Director, Book Acquisitions & Editing;* Susan Hills, *Senior Acquisitions Editor;* Julie Houtz, *Director, Book Editing;* Miriam Calderone, *Editor;* Thomas Lytle, *Creative Director;* Donald Ely, *Art Director;* Lisa Hill, *Graphic Designer;* Cynthia Stock, *Typesetter;* Kelly Marshall, *Production Manager;* Shajuan Martin, *E-Publishing Specialist*

Copyright © 2022 ASCD. All rights reserved. It is illegal to reproduce copies of this work in print or electronic format (including reproductions displayed on a secure intranet or stored in a retrieval system or other electronic storage device from which copies can be made or displayed) without the prior written permission of the publisher. By purchasing only authorized electronic or print editions and not participating in or encouraging piracy of copyrighted materials, you support the rights of authors and publishers. Readers who wish to reproduce or republish excerpts of this work in print or electronic format may do so for a small fee by contacting the Copyright Clearance Center (CCC), 222 Rosewood Dr., Danvers, MA 01923, USA (phone: 978-750-8400; fax: 978-646-8600; web: www.copyright.com). To inquire about site licensing options or any other reuse, contact ASCD Permissions at www.ascd.org/permissions or permissions@ascd.org. For a list of vendors authorized to license ASCD e-books to institutions, see www.ascd.org/epubs. Send translation inquiries to translations@ascd.org.

ASCD® is a registered trademark of Association for Supervision and Curriculum Development. All other trademarks contained in this book are the property of, and reserved by, their respective owners, and are used for editorial and informational purposes only. No such use should be construed to imply sponsorship or endorsement of the book by the respective owners.

All web links in this book are correct as of the publication date below but may have become inactive or otherwise modified since that time. If you notice a deactivated or changed link, please email books@ascd.org with the words "Link Update" in the subject line. In your message, please specify the web link, the book title, and the page number on which the link appears.

PAPERBACK ISBN: 978-1-4166-3130-9      ASCD product #122035      n7/22
PDF E-BOOK ISBN: 978-1-4166-3131-6; see Books in Print for other formats.
Quantity discounts are available: email programteam@ascd.org or call 800-933-2723, ext. 5773, or 703-575-5773. For desk copies, go to www.ascd.org/deskcopy.

**Library of Congress Cataloging-in-Publication Data**

Names: Schwanke, Jen, author.
Title: The teacher's principal : how school leaders can support and
    motivate their teachers / Jen Schwanke.
Description: Arlington, VA : ASCD, [2022] | Includes bibliographical
    references and index.
Identifiers: LCCN 2022008125 (print) | LCCN 2022008126 (ebook) | ISBN
    9781416631309 (paperback) | ISBN 9781416631316 (pdf)
Subjects: LCSH: Motivation in education—United States. | School
    principals—United States. | Educational leadership—United States. |
    Mentoring in education—United States. | Teacher-principal
    relationships—United States.
Classification: LCC LB2831.92 .S394 2022  (print) | LCC LB2831.92  (ebook)
    | DDC 371.2/012—dc23
LC record available at https://lccn.loc.gov/2022008125
LC ebook record available at https://lccn.loc.gov/2022008126

31 30 29 28 27 26 25 24 23 22          1 2 3 4 5 6 7 8 9 10 11 12

# The Teacher's Principal

## How School Leaders Can Support and Motivate Their Teachers

# Acknowledgments

I am exceedingly grateful to my rich network of colleagues and friends, and for the family that surrounds me with support and love: my sister, Leah, for her listening ear and genuine gladness when good things happen to other people; my parents, Carli Moorefield and Dan Moorefield, for always rooting me on; and to Carol Schwanke, for providing unending support in countless ways. All my love and appreciation to my beautiful children, Jack and Autumn, for giving me purpose. To my fabulous husband, Jay, I am overwhelmed with gratitude. Thank you for always helping me find laughter and balance.

Thank you to ASCD for supporting my work. Special thanks go to Susan Hills, who worked alongside me from the beginning concept to the final draft, and Miriam Calderone, who helped bring the book to life. I am grateful!

The inspiration for this book, and for the work I do every day, comes from teachers. I have been unspeakably lucky to spend my career alongside hundreds of phenomenal teachers. Although there are too many to individually name, I hope each one knows how they have touched, inspired, and motivated me throughout the years. Teachers are the backbone of our education system, and they deserve all the respect and appreciation we can give.

# Introduction

In my years working as a school administrator, I have spent a great deal of time trying to read the minds of teachers. What are they thinking? What inspires them, motivates them, makes them lose energy and faith in themselves? Of particular interest to me is learning how some teachers sustain their purpose over the course of a career while other teachers falter, lose focus, and become disinterested or apathetic. In those cases, I wonder if there is anything to be done to motivate them anew. Is there any way a principal can help teachers have as much enthusiasm in their last year of teaching as they had in the first year?

Although I'm not necessarily proud of the path that led me to teaching, I *am* very proud of having found my purpose and built a life as an educator. My journey to being a teacher started because, quite frankly, I couldn't think of anything else to do. I'd graduated early from college with a liberal arts degree. I was very young and had no real career prospects or life goals. Bartending paid the bills, but the late nights, fast-paced lifestyle, and aching joints were wearing me out. I felt old, and I hadn't even done anything yet. As a college English major, I'd been passionate about literature and writing, so when a late-night bar customer slurred, "You're wasting yourself here. You ought to teach English," I decided he might be right. I found my way to a master's program that offered a teaching certificate, applied to the university, and enrolled.

Although I was glad to have a path forward, my purpose for teaching was not strong. I loved literature and needed a sustainable way to pay rent—that was it. But my teacher certification program awoke something in me. With the help of a couple of passionate professors and two lucky student-teacher placements, my roots of purpose were planted, and soon I knew I'd found my life's work. When I landed my first teaching job, I happily immersed myself in a 60-hour workweek that included coaching two sports and advising two clubs. My students and I were on a mission. I was a sentence-diagramming, journal-reading, literature-spouting storm trooper. I was *all* in. I taught and coached my guts out. Having discovered my purpose, I prioritized my career and developed patterns that made me proud.

A teacher's life is long and circuitous. As my journey has evolved, my purpose, priorities, and patterns have changed and changed again. Sometimes, I've been exclusively focused on my work. Other times, such as when slammed by unexpected postpartum depression or mourning the suicide of a grandparent, I could barely get out of bed, let alone remember why I'd ever wanted to teach. I've gone through periods of being the first one in the school building in the morning and staying in my classroom until after dark to make evening check-in calls to students or parents. I've also gone through periods of sliding in at the bell and keeping an eye on the clock throughout the day, counting the minutes until I could go home again and hoping my students didn't notice my lack of energy. Sometimes, I'm certain I am engaged in my life's great work; other times, I feel like just another cog in a giant wheel. I've come to know that these changes are part of a cycle of work and life, and they are neither wrong nor right.

When I left teaching and became a principal, I began focusing my attention on teachers and watched the various ways they navigate a career that typically spans more than three decades. I've wondered, time and again, how a principal can ease the highs and lows of a teacher's career fluctuations. I've repeatedly asked myself, "What is it that really motivates teachers to be the best they can be?"

There are no easy answers. Research has revealed multiple motivating factors. One study by Catherine Sinclair (2008) found that student teachers enter the profession for a wide variety of reasons. In some cases, like mine, it is simply by default. Sometimes there are extrinsic motivations, such as an attraction to the social and creative nature of teaching, favorable working conditions, and the sort of life it might provide ("life fit"). For some, becoming a teacher seems an "easy" path to take or seems to offer some sort of professional status. Other times, student teachers enter the teaching profession for more intrinsic reasons. They want to work with children; they are attracted to the intellectual, personal, and professional development and stimulation; or they believe they have what it takes to be a good teacher.

One factor that doesn't show up much in research is the impact that a principal has on someone's decision to become a teacher. Although many teachers can't take their future principals into account when embarking on their careers, principals can still have a significant impact on their work in the classroom. I believe a principal can make teaching a positive and fruitful experience—or make it so miserable that a teacher's original purpose wavers and weakens.

In this book, I provide a practitioner's view of how a principal can stay connected to the teacher's experience by evaluating how purpose, priorities, and patterns drive a teacher's work. I explain the different ways in which these motivators are manifested, describe what they look and sound like, and provide examples of how principals can support teachers driven by each one. I also show how principals can monitor these motivations in their daily work, and how they can measure their success at connecting to teachers in this way.

In the next chapter, we'll get started by examining exactly how purposes, priorities, and patterns interact to motivate teachers— and how understanding this process can help principals create a culture where every teacher feels seen, heard, and valued.

# How Purpose, Priorities, and Patterns Motivate Teachers

*As you consider the complexities and culture of your school staff, you wonder how you can possibly help each teacher individually while also leading them together as a team. You want to create a culture focused on your students, and you want each teacher to feel valued, seen, heard, and respected. To ensure this, it will help to ask: What inspires your teachers most when they make decisions—purpose, priorities, or patterns?*

Many new principals make a pledge, upon leaving the classroom, to always remember what it was like to be a teacher. Unfortunately, the passage of time can dull those memories, making it difficult for veteran principals to truly slip into the minds and thoughts of teachers. It gets especially challenging when we are shouldering the discontent or frustration of our teachers, or when we are trying to lead with positivity in what can sometimes feel like a swamp of negativity. It's only natural to have moments where we think, "I would

5

*never* have behaved like that teacher is behaving" or "I just wish they'd stop complaining and get the work done."

But if we lose our connection to the teacher experience or forget to truly think like a teacher, we forgo opportunities to bring out the best in the teachers we lead. This is especially true today, as teachers are contending with challenges never before seen in education and having experiences many principals have never encountered: conflicts related to race relations, equity, and issues of inclusion; a global pandemic; political division and unrest; relentless scrutiny and criticism on social media. These days, being a school leader requires principals not only to *remember* their experiences as a teacher but also to *transcend* them. We must think about the teacher experience in racial, cultural, social, emotional, economical, and experiential contexts that are immeasurably different from those we may have experienced when we were teachers.

Fortunately, even if principals lack the background or schema to truly understand what motivates and drives teachers, they can still commit to leading by relying on empathy and the shared experiences that connect us. Students, classrooms, schools, and communities are all directly affected by the approaches teachers take to their work, and teacher performance reflects directly on the principal, who is accountable both *to* them and *for* them. In carrying that responsibility, it can be confusing for principals to figure out how, exactly, they should guide and help teachers through their journeys as educators, especially because each teacher has different needs. Those needs are dependent on personality, philosophy, work ethic, training, habits, routines, collegial influence, and so on. It is a principal's job to identify, acknowledge, and help meet those individual needs—regardless of their root cause.

But it's worth the investment. A principal's efforts to build positive, productive relationships with teachers can improve the entire culture of a school. It's simple, really: If teachers are doing well, students do well. If students do well, parents will be well. If parents are well, the community is well. And if all *that* is well, the principal has succeeded in leading a school effectively and with care. Which is why, when principals decide how to allocate their time, emotional energy, and physical resources, they should pour heavily into their support of teachers.

Like all human beings, teachers have layers of frailties. They act in surprising ways. Sometimes, they change and grow. Other times, they don't change a bit, staying stuck in a rut that resists growth. They get tired, energized, and tired again. They can simultaneously be loyal, disingenuous, kindhearted, rancorous, and generous. They carry powerful energy within and among themselves. Problems and issues can pop up without warning. When leading teachers, principals can feel as if they are merely reacting, seeking to find anteced-ents for teacher behaviors and patterns only *after* they've become a problem. This can lead principals to spend most of their time worrying about toxic or ineffective teachers, with very little emo-tional energy left to carry driven and effective teachers to greater excellence.

But what if principals could clearly identify potential antecedents or motivations for teachers' decision making? What if they could have a head start in deciding how to differentiate their support for teachers? What if all relationships between principals and teachers could be strengthened, thus improving the impact a principal has on teacher growth, instruction, and classroom effectiveness?

I believe that teachers' motivations can usually be found by examining their purpose, priorities, and behavioral patterns. Think of these as the three main parts of a tree, with purpose as the roots, priorities as the trunk, and behavioral patterns as the branches and leaves (see Figure 1.1).

# Purpose

Because purpose is the root system of teachers' work, it is not consistently visible—yet it is the deepest level of motivation for teachers. It serves to answer the question "Why am I an educator?" Many teachers are intrinsically motivated by deep personal beliefs about the power and value of education. They truly believe that having a positive impact on young people is the primary objective of their professional lives. Other teachers are driven more by extrinsic

---

**FIGURE 1.1**

# The Motivation Tree

## Patterns

Teachers' patterns are the visible habits and routines that drive their daily decisions. They are subject to frequent change and can be influenced by a principal's guidance and support. Patterns are supported by priorities and fed by purpose.

## Priorities

Teachers' priorities reveal how committed they are to student learning. They can shift throughout a teacher's career and are often divided between personal and professional priorities, which can affect one another. Priorities support patterns and are fed by purpose.

## Purpose

Teachers' purpose reflects their values and reasons for teaching. A positive purpose is driven by teachers' intrinsic belief in the value of student learning. It is the most fixed of the three motivators, rarely changing significantly throughout a career. Purpose feeds teachers' priorities and patterns.

---

factors like securing a steady job, following a safe and predictable career path, investing in a strong retirement system, or even having a built-in vacation every summer.

Having an intrinsic purpose is ideal, as it has been shown to impact a teacher's life and career in positive ways. For example, one study found that the higher teachers' intrinsic motivation, the higher their job satisfaction and the lower their stress (Davis & Wilson, 2000). In other words, if teachers have a strong purpose driven by an intrinsic belief in the importance of student learning, then external challenges won't bring them despair and anxiety. They can stay focused on their purpose because it comes from within. Teachers with a strong intrinsic purpose—what I refer to as *positive* purpose—tend to speak of students in a kind, gentle, and caring way and to believe that all students can succeed. They understand their role in developing the child as a learner, a thinker, and a lifelong problem solver. A positive purpose is an inside job. It is a personal and intimate part of who a teacher is.

When I think of purpose, I am reminded of a beloved local teacher who recently retired after almost four decades of teaching. She was almost inconsolable as she considered what her life would look like without "teacher" being part of her identity. In 39 years as a classroom teacher, she told me, she had never once given up on a child. "I know I will struggle with retirement," she fretted. "If I can't get up in the morning and think about improving a child's life, even in just a small way, I don't know who I am." I assured her that someone with her depth of purpose was bound to find fulfillment in other ways. Indeed, after her retirement, she became one of her school's most dedicated and trusted volunteers, helping in classrooms wherever she was needed and eventually launching a virtual read-aloud series that involved every student in the school.

Every teacher has a purpose story. I find it fascinating and insightful to ask teachers, "What brought you to this profession?" The answer usually goes one of two ways: either it leads to memories, connections, and stories outlining a path and purpose related to education, or it reveals a purpose that is detached from deeply held beliefs about student learning and more aligned to extrinsic motivators.

Of course, we'd all prefer a school full of intrinsically motivated teachers, but the reality is that some teachers—even effective ones—are more driven by external factors. Principals should understand that teachers with a *negative* purpose—those who are driven solely by external motivators unrelated to student learning—can become toxic to students and to the school environment. Even one disengaged or disinterested teacher can cause negativity to ripple throughout the entire school community. It is difficult to change a teacher with a negative purpose or an absent purpose, but the solution does not lie in simply ignoring the problem. Instead, principals can proactively seek to spark energy in even the most apathetic teacher.

# Priorities

Held up by the teacher's purpose, priorities form the core of a teacher's motivation. As Figure 1.1 shows, priorities are like the trunk of a tree—they are always visible, but they may recede into the background unless effort is made to really see them. Priorities are fed and anchored by purpose, and they in turn support and influence behavioral patterns. They drive teachers' daily decisions and define the actions they implement, year after year, as a part of their teaching practice—how kindly or patiently they interact with students, how well they know and embrace their curriculum, how deeply they connect with and commit to parents, and how vested they are in professional development.

Over time, priorities may shift based on a teacher's personal life changes (having a child, moving homes, caring for aging parents); professional challenges (teaching new content standards, adjusting to a new team member, struggling with technology upgrades); or environmental factors (a pandemic, safety concerns, disruptive student behaviors). Since priorities are not so deeply entrenched as purpose, and since they adjust with the cycles of life, it is inevitable that they will change over the course of a teacher's career—perhaps several times.

Some teachers reflect on changes in their priorities in a positive and healthy way, having learned to accept the ups and downs of life's demands. But other teachers may get anxious when they try to balance it all—and this is where a principal's reassurance and support can make a big difference. Shifts in priorities are understandable and common, and they can benefit teachers by making them more skilled at managing multiple priorities at once.

My own priorities shifted when I had children. No longer could I stay in my classroom long after dark, grading papers and planning ahead; instead, I had to hustle out of work to pick up my babies before the day care closed. Then, as my children grew, my priorities shifted again. My kids could be left at home for an hour or two after school, but they needed more academic support in the evenings. They became involved in extracurricular activities, which gobbled up my weekend time. Now that my children are a bit older, my priorities have shifted yet again. I have more free time, but it's much more unpredictable, as my kids have grown more social and immersed in very different interests. I am now less of a planner and more of a flexible parent and professional.

These gradual shifts in my priorities have helped me master the art of compartmentalizing my work. My job is still a huge part of what I do, but it's not *all* I do. My identity has expanded far beyond what it was before my priorities shifted. To the untrained eye, I may seem less dedicated than before, because I don't arrive at work before the sun rises and I don't stay until late at night. On busy "Mom" days, I arrive when the teachers arrive, and I leave when the teachers leave. This would have been unthinkable to me when I started my career; now, though, I see it as a wise and necessary balancing of priorities.

I believe that one of the best gifts principals can give teachers is to view priorities not as a hierarchy but as parallel boxes. Being an effective teacher should certainly be a priority—but so, too, should being a good friend, spouse, parent, or caretaker. One doesn't have to replace another. Priorities can coexist in peace, especially with effective time management and dedicated focus at the right times.

A dear friend of mine, Sara, is a respected and beloved teacher. Her priorities ebb and flow with her daily schedule. When she is teaching at school, she is intensely focused on each of the students in her room. When she leaves school, she supports her daughters' softball tournaments, travels to a neighboring state to visit her aging parents, and builds in time for dates with her husband, reading, watching reality television, and exercise. She attends professional development for a few weeks each summer, dives into books and resources about child development, and jumps on any new ideas she can implement in her classroom. School is not her only priority, but one of many. Because of her efforts toward accepting all her priorities as valued parts of her life, she is a balanced human being who lives with a sense of calm and peace that many of us would do well to emulate.

Of course, it's one thing for school to be one among multiple priorities, but quite another when it is no longer a priority at all. Some teachers—especially veterans who have learned how to take shortcuts—may find themselves shifting into a type of teaching autopilot. Teaching may become the last thing they think about—a way to pay the bills, but not a role with which they closely identify. In these cases, teachers are exhibiting what I refer to as *negative* priorities. Though principals may not know exactly where a teacher's priorities lie at any given time, they can notice when priorities are way out of whack and help teachers to balance them better.

# Patterns

In our metaphorical motivation tree, the branches and leaves represent the patterns of behavior a teacher presents to the world—the most visible evidence of what motivates them. They are the admirable traits in a strong teacher, and they are what dismay us in a weak teacher. Priorities can bloom and fade in cycles, and they can cause schoolwide problems if they aren't properly managed. Patterns of behavior may include when and how teachers plan each day's instruction, how they set up their classroom, how they handle discipline problems, and how quickly and thoroughly they provide student feedback. These patterns predict how a teacher will react to the small but recurring challenges in a school day—disruptions to schedules, angry parents, collegial relationship issues.

Patterns directly reflect a teacher's priorities. Just as positive priorities lead to positive patterns, negative priorities lead to negative patterns. Fortunately, negative patterns can be more easily disrupted than negative priorities, either intrinsically (by a teacher deciding to change) or extrinsically (by a nudge from a principal, or through collaboration with a mentor or colleague). Principals can help teachers to shift their patterns from negative to positive by adjusting their routines, offering a different instructional assignment, providing training or resources, or connecting them with effective colleagues with a positive purpose.

# Understanding Manifestations of Purpose, Priorities, and Patterns

Figure 1.2 shows a list of possible manifestations of negative or positive purpose, priorities, and patterns that teachers may exhibit, and provides potential action steps a principal might take to support or address them. This table offers an identification process and a path to navigating the "why" behind teacher performance and practices. Rather than saying, "That teacher is so lazy, I don't know what to

**FIGURE 1.2**

## Positive Versus Negative Purpose, Priorities, and Patterns

| POSITIVE | NEGATIVE |
| --- | --- |
| **PURPOSE** | **PURPOSE** |
| **Teacher Characteristics** | **Teacher Characteristics** |
| • Placing students first | • Being disengaged |
| • Advocating for students | • Being chronically absent |
| • Valuing family voices | • Showing apathy |
| • Handling crises well | • Exhibiting defiance |
| • Finding joy in the work | • Refusing to participate |
| • Staying energized | • Engaging in insubordination |
| • Modeling strong teaching | • Sabotaging leadership |
| • Making student-driven decisions | • Showing disdain for students |
| • Seeing the whole child | • Engaging in destructive criticism |
| **Principal Support** | **Principal Response** |
| • Hiring for purpose | • Discussing negativity honestly |
| • Connecting new teachers to mentors | • Providing alternatives |
| • Asking who benefits from decisions | • Shifting the environment |
| • Supplying timely, positive feedback with no strings attached | • Providing appropriate professional development |
| • Providing opportunities for shared leadership | • Digging for compassion |
| • Providing nonleadership opportunities | • Letting teachers go |
| • Showing constant and genuine appreciation | |

*(continued)*

14   •   The Teacher's Principal

FIGURE 1.2 (*continued*)

# Positive Versus Negative Purpose, Priorities, and Patterns

| POSITIVE | NEGATIVE |
|---|---|
| **PRIORITIES** | **PRIORITIES** |
| **Teacher Characteristics** | **Teacher Characteristics** |
| • Equanimity | • Detachment |
| • Dependability | • Annoyance and irritation |
| • Showing up | • Feeling overwhelmed |
| • Expertise | • Communicating poorly with parents |
| • Being excited by new instructional challenges | • Disinterest in professional development |
| • Reading students' records | **Principal Response** |
| • Extracurricular involvement | • Providing temporary flexibility and resources |
| • Engaging in professional development | • Expressing empathy |
| • Willingness to engage in necessary processes | • Shifting job responsibilities |
| • Thinking of every student's needs | • Modeling solution-based problem solving |
| • Accepting that "life happens" | • Encouraging support systems at school |
| **Principal Support** | |
| • Providing empathy, sympathy, and trust | |
| • Eliminating priorities that don't support student growth | |
| • Noticing, complimenting, and reinforcing | |
| • Seeking to understand | |
| • Listening closely to teacher feedback | |
| • Being proactive | |
| **PATTERNS** | **PATTERNS** |
| **Teacher Characteristics** | **Teacher Characteristics** |
| • Respecting protocol | • Excessive complaining |
| • Thorough and consistent instructional planning | • Neglecting colleagues |
| • Providing student choice, student voice, and evidence of learning | • Managing time poorly |
| • Connecting with students | • Carrying stress |
| • Responding to assessment data | • Poor planning |
| • Differentiating instruction | • Neglecting the classroom environment |
| • Pursuing innovation | • Disinterest in the roots of discipline problems |
| • Providing timely feedback | • Not providing feedback to students |
| • Communicating with parents | • Responding poorly to challenges |
| • Being on time | **Principal Response** |
| • Deflecting stress | • Going directly to the problem |
| **Principal Support** | • Starting with a conversation |
| • Establishing expectations | • Being honest and taking ownership |
| • Frequently and immediately acknowledging positive patterns | • Getting to the "why" |
| • Ditching rigid accountability measures | • Providing additional training and resources |
| • Monitoring teacher satisfaction | • Reviewing expectations |
| | • Distinguishing between negative patterns and mere annoyances |
| | • Sharing leadership (to a point) |
| | • Abiding by the Five *R*s |
| | • Encouraging teamwork, collegiality, and communication |

do to motivate him," a principal might say, "Although the teacher is showing a negative pattern of laziness, I know from my time working with him that he has a deeply rooted purpose for being a teacher. Have his priorities changed? What might I do to disrupt this apathetic pattern I'm seeing?" Or rather than saying, "That teacher is toxic," a principal might say, "There are toxic patterns emerging in this teacher, and she isn't prioritizing improvement. She may not have—or may have lost—a sense of purpose. How can I help her find her way?"

In the coming chapters, we will study how we, as principals, can celebrate teacher strengths or challenges by asking, "Is this a situation of purpose, priorities, or patterns?" When we let teachers know that we value purpose, understand the fluidity of priorities, and have particular expectations about patterns, we can empower them to take ownership of their motivations, ensure a more positive school culture, and provide a better learning experience for students.

# 2

# Building on Positive Purpose

*Miss R. is the teacher who comes to mind when you think*
*about purpose. Often, you will go days at a time without even*
*seeing her, because she's in her room, intent on working with*
*students and facilitating their learning. When you do see her,*
*she talks enthusiastically about her students; she is proud*
*to explain their growth and likes telling stories about their*
*personalities. She speaks of students who struggle with social-*
*emotional or behavioral issues with the same empathy and*
*focus she holds for high-achieving students. She is respectful of*
*each child, each parent, and each home environment.*

*"I love being a teacher," Miss R. says. "There are hard days,*
*and days I am so tired I can't think straight, but I can't imagine*
*doing anything else." Her colleagues respect her, because her*
*input on curricular and operational issues is always on point*
*and circles back to student needs. As her principal, you rarely*

*need to provide suggestions for instruction. In fact, you prefer
to just stay out of her way and let her work her magic. Your
only real challenge is to make sure you let her know how valued and appreciated she is as a member of your staff.*

As the metaphorical tree in Figure 1.1 (p. 8) shows, a teacher's purpose is the root system of motivation. Fortunately, most teachers
come to the teaching profession with a strong, student-centered purpose. They genuinely enjoy students and thrive when helping them
learn and grow. These teachers often become our secret (or not-
so-secret) favorites, because they are the ones who inspire others,
persevere through difficulty, truly appreciate their jobs, and scatter
good vibes wherever they go. These teachers are the easiest to lead.

Some teachers establish their positive purpose from the very
beginning. One of the most purpose-driven teachers I've ever
known—we'll call her Meesha—decided at age 3 that she would be a
teacher. "When my mother dropped me off at preschool, I fell in love
with my teacher," she told me. "She had beautiful hair and the kindest
smile I had ever seen. She smelled sweet, like graham crackers and
vanilla. There was a complete set of Lincoln Logs I could play with
anytime I wanted." On that very first day of school, Meesha thought
to herself, "*That's* what I'm going to do when I'm a grown-up."

Of course, it isn't always that simple or direct. Teachers can find
their purpose for teaching in many different ways. For some, it's by
having an inspiring high school teacher who incites a passion for a
particular content area. For others, it's a feeling of being "at home"
in a school setting. Some teachers find their way toward their career
while in college, attracted to a university's strong education program or a particularly influential advisor. Others decide to teach
after watching an inspiring movie about a teacher who truly made a
difference to students.

My father, now almost 75 years old, chose a rural life on an Ohio
farm after graduating from college, raising his family while working
as a contractor and hay farmer. But at age 40, he discovered a series
of books by special education teacher Torey Hayden that inspired

him to go back to graduate school and secure a teaching license. Hayden's books were lovely and moving accounts of her experiences working with students with autism, Tourette's syndrome, and selective mutism. Her writing highlighted the magic of teachers who stay committed, who stick around, who never give up on a child who needs them. Although my father ultimately chose not to become a second-career educator, he'd been deeply inspired by Hayden's work. Educators like Hayden can motivate potential teachers to find their life's passion. But regardless of the circumstances that bring teachers to a career in education, when they do so out of an intrinsic and focused desire to do right by young people, they ensure that their purpose will be rooted deeply enough to hold them up throughout the course of their professional lives.

Not all teachers are driven by a positive purpose based on their intrinsic beliefs about the value of student learning. Some may have joined the teaching profession for the job security, the retirement benefits, or the long break in June and July. Some of these teachers may show problems based on their purpose, but others will still do excellent work. Either way, principals will benefit from getting to know teachers on a "purpose level," because purpose explains why they come to work every day.

# Characteristics of Positive Purpose

Let's take some time to consider what a principal might notice and appreciate in teachers with a positive purpose.

## Placing Students First

Teachers with a positive purpose strive to answer the same question, time and time again: "What do my students need from me?" They don't allow adult problems or bureaucratic roadblocks to burden them. They look for solutions to support their learners, and they never stop believing students can and will succeed. If asked, "Why do you teach?" these educators would be perplexed by the question. It's obvious to them that there is only one reason: for their students.

## Advocating for Students

Teachers with a positive purpose will always advocate for students. They will stick up for students individually, through personalized interactions and exchanges, and find ways to do it on a larger scale, too. In team or department meetings, special education planning, and parent-teacher conferences, teachers with a positive purpose offer a perspective that consistently brings the conversation back to the student experience. Being a champion of students isn't always easy; teachers who do so sometimes encounter resistance, particularly if their advocacy makes things uncomfortable for colleagues or requires a change in practice. But teachers who advocate for students don't waver under pressure because they believe students will benefit from having a teacher's voice on their side.

Some 10 years after I'd left the classroom for the principalship, I was dining out with my family when our server recognized me. I'd been her 7th grade teacher almost 20 years prior. She'd changed quite a bit, but I could recognize the sweet and sassy glint in her eyes. At 13, she had often been in trouble. Even then, I'd sensed how burdened she was by the suspicion that most of her teachers didn't really *like* her. To be fair, she could be challenging—there were times when she presented rude, dismissive, even combative behavior. I'd felt a kinship with her, though, and tried to change her deeply held narrative that adults were not to be trusted. I asked for, and was reluctantly granted, permission to provide an alternative to detention when she ran into trouble. I offered to have her come to my room, where I could work with her or even just let her sit and read. Essentially, I gave up a semester's worth of my afternoon plan period to keep her with me.

At the time, she hadn't been grateful—relieved, maybe, but not grateful. To her, I was simply the lesser of two evils. But over the course of the semester, we developed an easy rapport and grew fond of each other. The next year, she moved on to high school and I transferred to a different middle school, so we lost touch.

I was thrilled to see her again in the restaurant. I introduced her to my family, and we caught up briefly.

"I want to thank you," she said. "I know all the things you did to keep me out of trouble." Her eyes welled up. "You were the only one who stuck up for me."

*Stuck up for me.* Those words landed like a thud in my gut. Doesn't *every* child deserve teachers who stick up for them? Advocacy for students, whether individual or collective, public or private, is an inherent characteristic of teachers with positive purpose—they do it without needing acknowledgment, gold stars, or public gratitude. They do it even when the advocacy is unpopular or leads to the difficult implementation of new systems or processes. They do it even when no one is looking.

## Valuing Family Voices

As we all know, parents and guardians have an enormous influence on a child's school experience. Teachers with a positive purpose invite a child's family to join the process of learning, recognizing the value of home-based connections in the child's educational journey. These teachers value the family's input and accept that parents and guardians know and love their children on an indescribable level. At the same time, purposeful teachers don't disparage families that are disengaged. They understand that a lack of input doesn't necessarily indicate neglect or apathy; parents may be busy, distracted, or uncertain how they can help. Many parents lack confidence; had negative school experiences when they, themselves, were children; or don't have the means to get involved. Teachers with a positive purpose focus on the student first, adding value through family input—however much the family can or wishes to give—in a way that is helpful for the child.

## Handling Crises Well

"In a crisis," John F. Kennedy once said, "be aware of the danger— but recognize the opportunity." Kennedy's recommendation reflects a tendency I see in teachers who are good at handling crises. This was never more evident than when the COVID-19 pandemic hit our schools. The power and fear of the virus took us by surprise, as did the swift lockdown restrictions that came with it. I was surprised, and often dismayed, to see wildly different responses from teachers. Some pouted and resisted. Some raged. Some took to social media to explain how and why they couldn't possibly do their jobs in these ridiculous conditions.

But others took a deep breath and got to work. They flipped their classrooms to remote learning environments over the course of one weekend. They taught themselves new technology platforms and started personalizing lessons to fit in various home learning environments. They started schlepping books and resources to their students' front porches. They made audio and video an integral part of their instruction. They replaced projectors with document cameras and added learning systems to their repertoires. These teachers were actively implementing their positive purpose. They didn't care that their jobs changed overnight. They simply changed, too, because they *just wanted to keep teaching*. That's why they stayed calm and effective when they suddenly became online teachers, when they had to adjust their lessons to be meaningful from behind a laptop screen, and when they had to begin communicating with parents in new and unexpected ways. They came up with solutions and saw the opportunity buried within the crisis.

Crisis takes on many forms for a teacher. It can originate with something seemingly small: a student's disruptive comment in class or refusal to engage in classwork; an unexpected technology failure; a resource that is suddenly unavailable. Teachers rooted in positive purpose can handle these small crises seamlessly and without fanfare. Colleagues, administrators, students, and parents often don't even know they happened. The teacher just deals with them, learns from them, teaches alongside them, and moves on.

But teachers also deal with life-shifting crises that affect them in deeply personal ways. Teaching through national or international calamities like mass shootings, political upheaval, racial tensions, or natural disasters can trigger crises that affect teachers in the classroom.

Here's an example. On January 6, 2021, students from all over the world watched as a Washington, D.C., protest turned violent and hundreds of protesters stormed the Capitol building. That evening, these students immersed themselves in news stories and social media posts about the incident. When they woke the next morning and joined their classmates at school, many wanted to talk about it, relying on teachers to serve as facilitators.

A friend of mine teaches advanced political science in high school. His students asked versions of just three questions: "How did the protestors get into the building?" "What would have happened if they had been Black?" and "Why do people follow dangerous leaders?" Deconstructing these questions led to weeks of excellent classroom discussion, and the teacher took great care weaving together historical and current events to deepen his students' thinking and broaden their perspective. He capitalized on this teaching opportunity with the help of his students' thoughtfulness, curiosity, and empathy. "My job was to be neutral while helping them form their own opinions," he told me. "They did the rest." But he deserves more credit than that. He took an external crisis and used it to improve his instructional content and expand his students' critical thinking and discussion skills.

This teacher's calm and confident approach to handling a complicated situation is a perfect example of teaching with a positive purpose. These teachers see the opportunity that lies within a teachable moment, and they don't waver in their goal to help students think, learn, and analyze both independently and in collaboration with others.

## Finding Joy in the Work

Teachers who approach their jobs with a positive purpose get a great deal of satisfaction from their work. They find joy when their students excel and don't let events out of their control bog them down. One study of more than 1,600 Australian teachers found that those who were motivated by internal beliefs about student attitudes and behaviors, student success, and building relationships with students reported high job satisfaction, whereas those who worried about extrinsic factors like increased expectations for schools, community opinion, media judgment, or the support of their leaders were the least satisfied (Dinham & Scott, 1996). Teachers with intrinsic purpose don't have to struggle to find happiness in their work. They know they're there to facilitate student growth—and when they see that growth, their purpose for teaching is validated.

It's easy to spot teachers who enjoy the work they do. They are the ones whose students thrive under their leadership. In their classrooms, there is contentment, curiosity, and satisfaction on the faces of both teacher and students.

## Staying Energized

We all know teaching isn't full of joy all the time. In fact, much of it can be a slog. I loved teaching, but still dreaded spending my weekends reading stacks of student writing, developing all sorts of mind tricks and self-rewards for grinding through.

"I sometimes struggle to get energetic and enthusiastic about teaching data analysis and probability," one veteran math teacher friend admitted to me. "I mean, *I* get tired of it, and I'm the *teacher.* Many days, I must fix my attitude before I start my day. And sometimes, after I begin teaching, it takes a few minutes before I start to feel the flow of excitement and energy. It's never as exhilarating as the first year, or even the second and third." Still, this teacher continues to find the positivity in her role, even if she needs to work at it a little more than she used to, because she has a positive purpose. "I genuinely love working with students and seeing them master concepts they'd thought they couldn't achieve," she told me. "It's fun. That's not to say it comes as easily as it did when I first started. But it always comes."

I've noticed that teachers with a positive purpose take occasional energy lulls in stride. They don't assume that being in a momentary rut means they no longer like their work; instead, they acknowledge the rut and move on. Ideally, they use any negative emotions they may feel in the moment to motivate a deeper dive into the work, which further supports and enhances their purpose.

## Modeling Strong Teaching

Teachers with a positive purpose are seen, heard, and discussed by students, parents, and admiring colleagues. As role models, they show the world what teachers can and should do. They plan extensively. They differentiate lessons. They flex and accept changes. They make it a priority to read their students' IEPs and evaluation reports. They review students' cumulative files yet are also always willing to give students a fresh start. By dedicating themselves to best instructional practices, they serve as exemplars of their profession.

## Making Student-Driven Decisions

Though there are no recent comprehensive studies capturing the number of decisions a teacher makes in a day, one 1968 study by researcher Phillip Jackson estimated that teachers have between 200 and 300 student interactions per hour—often unplanned or unpredicted, and usually calling for spontaneous decisions. Given the increased complexity of classroom teaching and the fact that teachers today are expected to differentiate instruction on the spot, we can assume that Jackson's estimate would be much higher today.

Teachers with a positive purpose naturally make decisions based on what their students need. Some decisions may involve diving into progress and achievement data and adhering strictly to curricular standards; others may involve stepping back from curriculum and engaging in activities to support social-emotional health. These teachers, driven by their intrinsic belief in the value of teaching, choose to make virtually all instructional and relational decisions with an eye to how students will benefit.

## Seeing the Whole Child

Teachers who were driven to education by internal values tend to actively seek positive relationships with students. This doesn't just mean having a good rapport with students, but also seeing every child individually and noticing the hidden spark within.

I am fortunate enough to work with many teachers who, when asked about any student in their classroom, can immediately tell me all about that unique child—traits related to their friendships, socialization, academics, family, habits, talents, and areas for growth. These are the teachers who don't lead with negativity like "Well, he just can't keep up" or "He's just not able to do the work." Instead, they describe students in terms of how they fit in the classroom, what types of activities they might like, how their home environment affects their learning, how they add to the classroom community. Teachers with a positive purpose know each child's story, helping them create a connection that extends far beyond the curriculum.

# Supporting Teachers with Positive Purpose

Now that we have described some of the traits that characterize teachers with a positive purpose, let's talk about how a principal can support and empower them. As I mentioned earlier, teachers with positive purpose are the easiest to lead, especially when they are also independent problem solvers. Having a school full of teachers with positive purpose would be lovely, but it might drive the principal out of a job—after all, there would be very few problems to solve, right? Actually, no: principals still have a prime role to play supporting these teachers so they can do their best work.

In their study on principal efforts to empower teachers, Davis and Wilson (2000) did find that teachers who are internally driven to do good work do not change their motivation based on a principal's actions. But this doesn't mean a principal should ignore or dismiss the needs of the strongest teachers. In fact, principals would do well to allocate as much time and energy to teachers with a positive purpose as they do to others, because even the strongest educators flourish in a welcoming, warm environment of collegial energy, positive feedback, and professional development that challenges and excites them. Even the most confident and independent teachers appreciate feedback, validation, and encouragement from their leaders. With all of this in mind, here are some examples of ways principals can help teachers solidify and enhance their positive purpose.

## Hiring for Purpose

Many districts use a standardized screening tool for initial hiring interviews. Such tools can be remarkably effective at creating a pool of candidates with positive purpose. However, these programs also contain loopholes that can be difficult to close. Sometimes candidates are coached to give "correct" answers, so they say what they think the interviewers want to hear rather than what they actually believe. Indeed, many university programs actively and explicitly train their graduates to answer interview questions with words and phrases that imply positive purpose.

Several years ago, I was asked to conduct interviews at a job fair at a nearby university. I brought a list of initial standard questions, opening with two that were intended to reveal a teacher's purpose. It wasn't long before I noticed a clear pattern in candidate answers. At the end of the day, I'd conducted almost 20 interviews, and every single candidate had responded to my two "purpose" questions in an eerily similar way.

First question: "Why did you want to be a teacher?"

Twenty candidates: "I just love seeing the lightbulb go off when a student really understands what I've been teaching."

Next question: "Tell me about your philosophy of teaching."

Twenty candidates: "I think it's really important to set high expectations, but also to differentiate instruction according to each student's needs."

I imagined the seminar class where a professor told students how to prepare for the interviews: "They'll ask you why you want to be a teacher. When you answer, definitely mention a lightbulb. And if they ask about philosophy, make sure to mention two key terms: *high expectations* and *differentiation*." The experience was disheartening. None of the candidates seemed to have genuinely reflected on their purpose—they were only focused on getting a job.

Of course, just because candidates respond to interview questions with contrived answers doesn't mean their résumés should be immediately discarded. Every candidate deserves consideration, and interviewers can look beyond rote answers by asking deliberate follow-up questions that will reveal trends in purpose, like these:

- Tell me how you get that lightbulb moment. Does this come through whole-class lesson planning, or through individual instruction? Do you have any examples?

- You mentioned you love seeing a child understand a concept. Who is responsible for a child's learning?
- When a student doesn't understand a concept, do you lower your expectations to ensure they are successful? Why or why not?
- Can you explain how "high expectations" and "differentiated instruction" will coexist in your classroom?
- How do pre-assessments help you differentiate your instruction? In what other ways can you decide what each learner might need from you?

In addition to conducting interviews, principals can watch videos of a candidate teaching, conduct in-person visits and extensive reference checks, evaluate past experiences, and consider anything else that seems relevant to uncovering a candidate's purpose. When you find a candidate whose purpose is deeply rooted and genuinely positive, you can be confident that you're investing in a long-term relationship with a teacher who is there for the right reasons.

## Connecting New Teachers to Mentors

New teachers bring an enthusiasm to school that is contagious and inspiring. I love watching them "nest" in their classrooms, working hard to get everything just as they want it. After a standard onboarding process, I try to stay out of the way, because they tend to have all the gusto they need on their own. But one thing I do with intention is connect them with esteemed veteran colleagues, because new teachers can really bloom when surrounded with mentors who have similar levels of strength and conviction. Providing and creating a mentoring network for new teachers is a surefire way to solidify their purpose. As Sehgal, Nambudiri, and Mishra (2017) write, working alongside peers who provide reinforcement and feedback "can positively influence a teacher's intrinsic motivation and his/her perception about his/her competence" (p. 512). In other words, after hiring for purpose, we should *surround* teachers with purpose.

Many schools have formal programs in place to pair new teachers with a mentor, outlining clear expectations for consistent meetings between the two parties. New teachers and mentors follow a pre-scribed set of orientation and onboarding activities. Perhaps more valuable, though, are less formal mentoring scenarios.

When I was first hired as a teacher, my principal was very deliberate about making these kinds of scenarios happen. The first year I worked for her, she made several seemingly casual comments about other teachers. "You'll find Mr. D. to be an expert in working with challenging students," she told me after a student with volatile behaviors was placed in my class. "I hope you'll find time to get to know him." Another time, in a conversation about finding challenging literature resources for my students, she said, "Ms. B. knows the English curriculum like the back of her hand. I think she would be happy to sit down with you and help you find the perfect resources for your planning." Her breezy, casual tone belied her intentions—and it worked. I made time to get to know the teachers my principal admired. This kind of informal professional matchmaking on the part of principals can be an excellent investment in the future.

## Asking Who Benefits from Decisions

Wouldn't it be nice if we could start over and hire only teachers with positive purpose? Unfortunately, that's not how it works. We inherit someone else's hires and a pre-existing staff, often made up of teachers who have been there for years. What we *can* do, though, is help lead staff toward a culture of positive purpose.

I've watched principals do this by taking great care with the decisions they make and the language they use. They refer to students in a way that makes it clear that their school has a "students first" culture. For example, I once worked with a principal who would ask her staff, "Are we making *teacher* decisions or *student* decisions?" The question sometimes rankled teachers, because they recognized that if she was taking the time to ask it, a "teacher decision" had probably been made. That didn't mean the decision was detrimental to students, necessarily, but the *origin* wasn't based on student benefit.

I've adopted this principal's technique in my own decision making. I'll ask myself, "Are you pushing for this particular resolution because it benefits students, or because it benefits the adults who work with them?" Sometimes both parties benefit, making it a win-win situation. But if only the adults do, it might be helpful to go back and revisit the decision.

## Supplying Timely, Positive Feedback with No Strings Attached

Years ago, when I first started as a principal, I received feedback from our Human Resources department that felt like a criticism: I was "giving" too many teachers high performance evaluations. The thinking, it seemed, was that my cumulative evaluation ratings should reflect a bell curve, with most teachers falling into the middle two rankings ("improving" and "skilled") and just a few at the lowest ("developing") and highest ("accomplished") extremes. Although I understood the value of being conservative with high rankings, I simply didn't believe teacher performance needed to follow a bell curve. After all, don't we want as many teachers as possible on the "accomplished" side of our rubric? With appropriate support, professional development, and mentoring, wouldn't a massive tilt toward "accomplished" reflect strong leadership and an effective school?

I thought about it a lot, asking myself to be open-minded, but I kept getting stuck on two things. The first was my suspicion that formal evaluations do very little to change a teacher's actual instructional planning, especially if the teacher finds the evaluation process to be a negative experience. And indeed, research does show that some evaluation tools do very little to change practice. For example, in her 2016 doctoral study of one state's performance evaluation tool, Dr. Jara Packer, a colleague and friend, examined the impact of teacher evaluations and found that only one out of ten factors seemed to have the ability to change teacher behavior—and that factor was related to the classroom environment, not actual instruction. Knowing about these limitations, I saw no value in forcing my evaluation ratings to fit into a prescribed distribution.

The second thing I got stuck on was the implication that I was giving teachers high rankings without also providing them with constructive feedback. I resented this assumption. Everyone can benefit from constructive feedback, and it doesn't have to come from a place of criticism. If a teacher does excellent work, we should say so, and we should document it using the formal evaluation tool given to us.

I've found I am best able to have rich and productive conversations about a teacher's professionalism, planning, and goals *after* I've celebrated the teacher's excellence formally and in writing. In other words, I strive to make teacher evaluations an opportunity to confirm a teacher's excellence, not to poke holes in it. Of course, I address areas of weakness, too, but not in a way that dismantles confidence. I speak as a collaborator rather than a punitive "boss." After all, working collaboratively with teachers has been shown to increase teacher efficacy (Sehgal et al., 2017). If the principal thinks a teacher is excellent, the teacher is more likely to be excellent. What's wrong with that?

The last thing I want is for effective teachers with positive purpose to dread their evaluations. When teachers work with their hearts and minds firmly rooted in positive purpose, it's our responsibility to acknowledge their efforts and show how much we appreciate them.

## Providing Opportunities for Shared Leadership

Even teachers with positive purpose may experience times when they aren't especially motivated or enthusiastic about their work. Principals might consider these moments opportunities to help teachers expand their professional footprint by sharing leadership responsibilities with them.

In a 2008 study, Wahlstrom and Louis reviewed the research on the impact of shared leadership between principals and teachers and found that principals who were willing to share the work helped teachers by "creating greater motivation, increased trust and risk taking, and building a sense of community and efficacy among its members" (p. 467). So even if teachers experience periods of stagnancy, they can often be nudged back into action by taking on new professional challenges.

When I began my career as an administrator, I felt I needed to own all leadership decisions. It was a heavy weight to carry. One day, frustrated by a lack of progress, I called a colleague. "I feel like I'm working harder than anyone else," I said. "I'm trying to roll out a new curriculum initiative, but no one on the staff seems to care."

"Have you asked for their input?" he asked.

"Well, no," I admitted. "I want to keep this off their plates. But if they would just try it out, I'm sure they'd appreciate what I'm trying to do."

He laughed out loud. "How insulting to them," he said.

I sputtered. "Insulting? I'm not trying to insult them. I'm trying to help."

"Take a moment and think that through," he said. "You lead a staff that collectively has hundreds of years of experience, insight, and perspective. Why don't you make them part of the process? Why not give them decision-making power? Have them identify where change and improvements need to occur. Not only will your initiative be more effective, but you'll gain two other things. First, they will 'buy in,' and they will work hard to make the initiative a success. Second, you won't be working harder than anyone else. You'll all be in it together. Success or failure won't be on your shoulders alone. You'll share it with people who created it."

He was right. When I let go—releasing leadership to the power and ingenuity of strong and capable teachers—it simultaneously made me a better leader and empowered the teachers to become better versions of their best selves. Using teachers to help with committee and department work, or getting their input in making curriculum, innovation, technology, and operations decisions, is a win-win for everyone involved.

## Providing Nonleadership Opportunities

It's important to note that not all teachers want to be leaders. In fact, some are repelled by the idea, because they associate leadership with conflict, trouble, and tension. In these cases, it's not necessary to nudge a teacher into a leadership role. There are other ways to highlight their excellence, starting with asking them what they want or need: "Is there an opportunity you're interested in that I haven't recognized? Is there anything I can do to help you achieve any goals?"

Two years ago, I asked those questions of one of my most revered and purposeful teachers, a quiet and unassuming model of teaching excellence. She responded that she wanted to help students struggling with social-emotional issues, so I suggested she attend training to lead a prospective school club for teenage girls with friendship challenges. She took the training and ended up facilitating the club, which now stands as both a by-product and a symbol of a teacher with rock-solid positive purpose who found a new way to contribute to students.

## Showing Constant and Genuine Appreciation

When I present to school leaders, I often leave them with this thought: if you think you're saying "thank you" enough, you're about halfway there. This message seems to resonate with leaders, inspiring them to double down on showing teachers how much they are valued. I call this "gratitude feedback." Even if we feel we are saying "thank you" a lot, there are likely many teachers who haven't heard from us in a while. "Hey, I really appreciate all you do" is one way to say it, but more specific feedback related to specific student growth can mean even more. Giving detailed gratitude feedback will feel welcome to even the most confident and rooted teacher. Here are some examples:

- Instead of saying "Thanks for all you do," say something like this: "I notice you are here early every single morning, and I see the results of your careful planning. You seem to really know your students, and the model of differentiation you've set up in your classroom is a model for how to serve each child's individual needs."
- Instead of saying "You go above and beyond," say something like this: "I want to recognize the extra effort you put into making our school such a positive place. Not only are you the liaison for our PTO, but you have some of the best RTI plans I've ever seen. I want to thank you for your willingness

to go beyond your job responsibilities. We wouldn't be 'us' without you."

- Instead of saying "You seem to be a lifelong learner," say something like this: "I appreciate your commitment to learning this new computer program. It's amazing how quickly you have learned what it can do and adopted it in your curriculum work. I love seeing you tackle new challenges, and I notice how your colleagues naturally follow your example."
- Instead of saying "You are really good at managing student behaviors," say something like this: "You've single-handedly made a difference in Bradlee's behaviors and engagement. I have noticed the reduction in outbursts and can see how eager he is to commit to learning. This is all due to your focus on his success and the research you've conducted on behavior antecedents."
- Instead of saying "Thanks—that was a great IEP meeting," say something like this: "When you lead IEP meetings, they work so smoothly and efficiently. I appreciate the front-loading you do with parents, and you really solidify the team of support staff. Your development and articulation of student goals are spot-on and a comfort to anxious parents. I really enjoy being in IEPs with you!"

Teachers can sense inauthentic measures of appreciation, so committing to genuine, detailed, timely, and relevant gratitude feedback is a surefire way to strengthen and sustain their purpose over the years. Of course, it gets more challenging when teachers don't have a positive purpose to begin with. In the next chapter, we will shift our focus to teachers who exhibit characteristics of negative purpose and examine how principals can help them contribute positively to the school community.

# 3

# Addressing Negative Purpose

*Mr. P. slips in and out of school unnoticed most days. He keeps to himself, but his colleagues complain that he leaves the building during every free period to run errands or, so the rumor goes, to work out at a nearby gym. After he turns in his check-out materials at the end of each school year, he is unavailable until the precise date teachers are expected to report back to the building. His students openly talk about his class being an "easy A." His expectations for student progress are low, and it's hard to decipher the intentions, if any, behind his instructional decisions. He is pleasant and does not cause visible conflict, but he avoids all extraneous effort toward schoolwide initiatives, and his colleagues resent his elusiveness.*

*After school hours, Mr. P. runs a successful rental-property business. "I'm just teaching for the retirement system and insurance benefits," he once told a colleague. "As soon as I'm*

*vested enough, I'm out of here and you'll never see me again."*
*Knowing that Mr. P.'s purpose does not align with students and*
*their needs, you wonder how to motivate him to invest more*
*time and energy into his students and the school.*

In the previous chapter, we discussed how principals can support the work of teachers with positive purpose. Teachers who are motivated intrinsically to work hard for students are role models for others, creating and sustaining a culture of excellence throughout a school.

In contrast, when a teacher's purpose is negative, everything else suffers. Most notably, the student experience is directly affected by the teacher's apathy or cynicism. Purpose affects how teachers prioritize their work duties and influences the patterns that drive their daily decision making. Although it is difficult for a principal to change a teacher's purpose, it can be done, especially with the gifts of time, patience, and judgment-free support.

Ideally, schools have very few teachers with a truly negative purpose because they tend to be weeded out through university programs and the hiring process. In spite of these safeguards, we have all had our share of teachers who just didn't want to be there. These are the teachers who are merely putting in time, collecting a paycheck, investing in retirement, counting the days until they can do or be something else. Returning to our motivation tree in Figure 1.1 (p. 8), we can imagine a negative purpose represented by thin and weak roots that cannot possibly continue to feed a teacher's career through inevitable challenges and changes.

It is disheartening for me to write about teachers with negative purpose, because I prefer to believe—as many principals do—that I can spark positive purpose in teachers if I just say the right thing, implement the right plan, or figure out how to properly motivate them. Unfortunately, it's not so simple. Although I've found I can usually unlock positive change in teachers who are struggling with priorities or patterns, this is difficult to do if a teacher is in the profession for the wrong reasons. That's a hard truth for principals to accept, especially those of us who observe, as I do, that it seems to take more effort to be miserable at work than to be pleasant and positive. For me, it isn't a big ask to feel—and express—gratitude for having a steady job where I can make a legitimate difference in the lives of a new generation. Wouldn't it just be easier to be cheerful, to enjoy the experience of being around young people, to find fulfillment, laughter, and satisfaction in working with learners?

Not necessarily. For those with negative purpose, there is limited motivational value to being an excellent teacher. And for the principals who lead them, it can be maddening to see the repercussions in the classroom.

Every profession has employees whose negative purpose cripples their productivity. It's a natural and expected part of management—despite our best efforts to inspire, all leaders have experienced some level of difficulty motivating some members of their teams. Yet principals tend to feel uniquely alone in facing this challenge, because often we are "stuck"—for years on end—with teachers whose negative purpose affects so many other components of our work. It can be exhausting, and the stakes seem especially high because of the direct impact teachers have on students and their visibility to parents and others in the community.

My friend Raku, who was a principal for many years, used to call me to brainstorm solutions for working with a particularly toxic teacher—we'll call her Ms. R.—whose primary purpose, it seemed, was to complain and create anxiety in everyone around her. Raku retired recently, and as he left the building for the last time, he felt like weeping. "Not because I was sad," he admitted. "I was overcome with relief. I was so glad that I didn't have to wake up one more day and wonder how much trouble Ms. R. would cause in my job."

This one teacher—just one—had been so consistently nasty and disruptive that Raku had spent countless hours of his professional life trying to sort out all the microaggressions she'd inflicted on students and colleagues. Nothing was so egregious that he could try for termination, and he probably wouldn't have been successful anyway. "She was brilliantly passive in her behavior," he said. For example, she would use a condescending and disrespectful tone when talking with students. "The actual words she used seemed appropriate, even kind," Raku said. "So when I recorded them on paper, there didn't seem to be a problem. It's hard to quantify or explain her *tone*. She would pull a student in for a conversation about his progress. The student would walk away feeling terrible, but when questioned about it, Ms. R. would grow indignant: 'What? I'm just trying to help!'"

A few months after his retirement, Raku reflected on the impact Ms. R. had had on him, on his students, and on his school.

"For years, I walked around with a low-grade anxiety because of this one teacher," he said. "There were usually one or two larger incidents a year in Ms. R.'s room, and those were awful, but my anxiety came from the countless tiny ones—the lack of effort she put into her instruction, the sarcastic way she talked to students, her refusal to give students feedback, an unidentifiable grading system, and an overburdening of homework, tests, and retakes. I never knew what the next problem would be, and until I retired, I hadn't acknowledged how heavily this problem weighed on my mind."

Raku had tried implementing plans and setting up structures to solve the problems, but Ms. R. ignored them, denied that a problem existed, or involved the teachers' union in accusing Raku of harassment. The entire school tiptoed around Ms. R., including Raku. "I knew she didn't want to be there, and I was never going to change that," he told me, shaking his head. He's not proud that he wasn't able to do anything about Ms. R.'s negative purpose. "I left it for the principal who replaced me," he said. "All I can do is hope my replacement was able to manage her better than I did." This, perhaps, is what haunts Raku the most—that despite his numerous efforts to find solutions, he'd left a mess for someone else to tackle.

Fortunately, teachers like Ms. R. are quite rare. All of us struggle with motivation at some point in our careers, but rarely to the extent that Ms. R. did. She represents a tiny portion of teachers—those who genuinely don't or can't make their work meaningful to them and who seem to enjoy spreading their misery to others. We can be thankful that most teachers without a strong positive purpose have found ways to be competent and relatively effective at school.

Before deconstructing characteristics of negative purpose, let's keep two things in mind. First, having a negative purpose doesn't necessarily indicate an intent to do harm. Rather, it might reflect apathy or detachment. Teachers might settle into their work mechanically, seeing it as "just a job" rather than a life's calling. Over time, these teachers might grow increasingly negative and resentful about the challenges, changes, and interruptions caused by their workload, their teaching environment, or their students. They might count the days until their retirement and be unapologetic about their disengagement from students and the school community. It's a slow burn, but again, it rarely begins as an intentional or malicious decision.

Second, it's important to note that a negative purpose can look a lot like negative priorities (see Chapters 4 and 5), but the two are actually very different. I have observed that negative purpose behaviors can linger for years, becoming part of a teacher's identity rather than a brief or uncharacteristic shift in behaviors. Teachers with negative purpose develop traits that are very difficult to change, which distinguishes them from teachers who are merely struggling with priorities or patterns.

# Characteristics of Negative Purpose

"Why are you a teacher?" Years ago, when I first started teaching, it was a long-running joke for teachers to answer that question with a quippy "Well, *obviously*, it's for June, July, and August." Fortunately, that answer was met with such dismay and embarrassment by parents, students, and colleagues that most teachers have abandoned it, even as a joke. But there are many other ways teachers with negative purpose may answer that question—all valid and justifiable: "I wanted to have children of my own, and this is a great job for a parent"; "I wanted to have the same school breaks as my children"; "My parents and grandparents were teachers." Teachers might also cite the typically steady retirement systems, the perception of a balanced life, or the security of having a job in a profession as old as time.

For many, these reasons are perfectly acceptable and can, of course, still lead to a positive teacher-student experience. For others, unfortunately, negative purpose can turn a teacher toward traits that are damaging to the students they are charged with helping. To better understand and help these teachers, let's consider some common characteristics of negative purpose.

## Being Disengaged

Teachers with negative purpose might avoid tasks that require a lot of effort and become detached from school, department, or team activities. If encouraged to participate, they may do so grudgingly or, worse, with an approach that feels like sabotage. These teachers leave on the last day of school and "disappear" for the summer—not necessarily because they have other priorities to take them away, but because they don't see value in staying connected with the school community. When not at work, they may refuse to check email, attend professional development, or respond to parents. Teachers with a negative purpose are well aware of their job's minimum requirements and hover near the lowest bar of expectation.

One common way that teachers manifest disengagement is by refusing to stay up-to-date on information affecting their students or the school community. Principals often send emails or host regular meetings to keep teachers aware of any new developments affecting their daily work, and when teachers ignore these, it can be incredibly frustrating.

A principal friend of mine sends an email every Friday with bulleted updates. Two of her teachers never even open it. "I understand they may not want to hear from me," she said. "But there is a lot of good stuff in those emails—things they really need to know. When they don't keep up with communications, they don't understand the rationale behind decisions, and they miss important events. And then they complain, 'No one told me.' It's hard on their team members, too, when one staff member never knows what is going on." This principal feels that all teachers should share responsibility for the smooth operations of the building by keeping up with communications. "When they refuse, I can't help but think they aren't there for the right reasons," she said.

## Being Chronically Absent

A colleague of mine has a teacher on staff who is absent every Friday. Week after week, he reports illness late Thursday evening. This teacher is in the twilight of his career now, but over his first 25 years as a teacher, he accumulated a great deal of sick time, and he has made up his mind to retire with a sick day balance of zero. Never mind the risk of "burning" all those sick days and needing them later, should he or someone he loves fall ill; never mind the misunderstanding he seems to hold about the intended purpose of sick days. Instead, this teacher is staunchly committed to missing as many days of work as he can. His four-day weeks have been damaging to his students, who struggle with a swinging door of substitutes at the end of each week. They've also damaged the morale of his fellow teachers. They all know he is not ill every Friday, and they look to the principal to call out his dishonesty. But the principal's hands are tied; the district's contract prohibits her from requesting a medical excuse from the teacher's doctors, and her multiple sit-down conversations with him have ended poorly. The teacher just shrugs, quotes the contract, and rolls his eyes when the principal pleads that his students need him. It's an ongoing clash of beliefs and purpose. "He's giving us all a bad name," a teacher in the building told the principal. "He's the kind of person who makes the public think teachers have it easy." The principal agrees, but there is little she can do to change the teacher's behavior. "He just doesn't *care*," she told me. "His purpose is not just absent—it's like he's operating with detrimental purpose."

When a teacher consistently misses a great deal of school for reasons unrelated to legitimate life challenges, this may indicate negative purpose—especially if the teacher doesn't seem to care about the consequences. These are teachers who feel frequent substitutes are perfectly reasonable stand-ins.

Another principal told me about a teacher nearing retirement who had a scheduled surgery with a 10-week recovery every single year—for five straight years. They were all elective surgeries, and all scheduled for the middle of March—so timed just right for her to miss the rest of the year. The principal had to approve the teacher's 10-week absence every year, even when the teacher ran out of medical leave days and switched to unpaid leave. "I kept thinking, she'll either run out of body parts or she'll finally retire," he joked. Ultimately, it was the latter, not the former, that took her out of the classroom.

## Showing Apathy

Though it's not as visible or damaging as chronic absence, apathy among teachers with a negative purpose can also be a problem. A colleague of mine worked with a teacher who relied exclusively on videos as instructional tools, followed by "quizzes"—worksheets she'd created to align with the videos. When the students turned in the worksheets, the teacher did a trade-and-grade, with peers grading each other's work and announcing the score aloud for the teacher to input into the computer's system. When asked to stop this practice, the teacher acquiesced—by skipping over the grading step altogether. In a show of defiance, she would distribute the worksheets and ask students to submit them in a tray that happened to be near the trash can. One student reported to her parents, who reported to the principal, that the teacher simply trashed the worksheets at the end of the week—without even looking at them—and all students went home with $A$ grades. The principal spoke to her, but she just shrugged. "What's the big deal? Everyone is happy, right? All parents want is the $A$. Nothing else matters. I'm fine being the teacher who gives the 'easy $A$.'"

Apathy doesn't necessarily indicate a lack of care and concern. I believe apathetic teachers don't deliberately seek negative experiences for their students; they just don't adopt the power or processes to provide positive experiences. A principal from a neighboring state once told me he'd walked in on a teacher assigned to oversee a study hall and found him sound asleep. The students were all tittering and giggling, excited at the potential drama that might come of the principal's visit. The principal looked at one of the students, who confided in a whisper, "He does this every day. We just let him sleep." Appalled, the principal woke the teacher. Later, in his office, he tried to offer an "out" to the teacher—was he feeling OK? Did he need some time off? Was there a reason he was so exhausted?

"Nah," the teacher shrugged. "It's just . . . well, it's just *study hall*."

"But you're supposed to be helping them with schoolwork!" said the principal. "And that's not even the worst of it. Something could happen! You're in charge! You're supervising!"

Another shrug from the teacher. "Ahhh, come on. It doesn't matter," he said. "They're good kids. They'll be fine."

While this may be an extreme example, any teacher who isn't fully engaged in supporting students' academic, social, and emotional development is showing the apathy of negative purpose.

## Exhibiting Defiance

To justify their subpar performance, teachers with a negative purpose might snub the processes and systems that are meant to support and protect them. Often they'll use negative or disparaging comments, refusal, or absenteeism to defy the school's mission.

A colleague of mine, the principal of a middle school, implemented a social-emotional student support program in which teachers would serve as advisors for students in a biweekly class period. One of his teachers was so incensed by this "additional prep" that he simply called off work every day the advisory period was scheduled. He defied the school's work by simply removing himself from it.

Instead of reacting with anger, the principal chose to respond with compassion, setting up a meeting to talk with the teacher to determine if there was something deeper that was concerning him.

"I thought there might be something bothering him about the program," the principal said. "Although I knew it was unlikely, I actually hoped his defiance was, in some way, a decision to defend students. Unfortunately, it wasn't anything that noble. He just shrugged and said, 'It looks like too much work.' That's when my suspicions were confirmed. He wasn't doing it because he didn't *want* to do it."

## Refusing to Participate

Refusal closely resembles defiance as a tactic, with negative purpose teachers refusing to participate in initiatives or schoolwide systems even if they have been mandated.

When a principal friend of mine made schedule changes to increase efficiency during student lunch hours, one of her teachers simply refused to accept them. "No way. I'm out," the teacher said. "It's just another flash in the pan. I'm just not going to participate. It'll go back to the old way soon enough."

My principal friend was stunned. She didn't want to formally reprimand the teacher, knowing it would cause ripples of strife within her staff and a showdown with union leadership, but she also knew that her new initiative—certain to solve a long-standing problem—couldn't work without teacher buy-in. She struggled to understand why all the other teachers seemed to like the idea and were willing to invest in its success while this one teacher simply refused.

She met with the teacher to gain insight about her refusal, even asking if she had any suggestions or ideas to make the initiative a success. "I can understand that this might help with efficiency, but I don't think it will last," the teacher said. "I'm not going to be part of it." In the end, the principal found a way to make the initiative work without this teacher's help, but she remains disappointed that a teacher refused to be part of a potential solution. "It's like she forgot the reason she's here," my friend said. Indeed.

## Engaging in Insubordination

In the spring of 2020, when COVID-19 forced schools to shut down, a principal I'd known for years called me, panicked. "I have a teacher who refuses to begin online instruction," he said.

"Refuses?"

"Yes! She says she just won't do it."

The entire district, state, nation—indeed, the entire globe—had shifted to remote learning within just a few days' time, but this particular teacher seemed to think she should be the exception. She claimed to have no training or adequate support to shift to online instruction. "No one has training or support," my friend moaned.

"But she is accusing me of negligence, saying I didn't prepare for this scenario, and it's *my* negligence, she says, that prohibits her from teaching her students. She feels I should get a substitute for her class until she receives adequate training."

"But a substitute wouldn't know these things either," I said.

"Exactly."

"She can't just . . . *refuse* to *teach*," I said. "No one expects online instruction to be perfect the first week, or even the first few weeks. All teachers will be learning new techniques, and there will be enormous collegial support for remote instruction."

"I've told her all that," he said. "She still refuses. She says she will not teach in an online environment."

"Well, then, it's a different word," I said. "It's *insubordination*." The teacher's defiance of authority and refusal to comply with orders was more severe than the actions we've previously discussed in this chapter. Insubordination crosses into different territory because it is a refusal to follow direction in ways that may result in denying students a fair and appropriate education. Insubordination will likely prompt intervention and support from a Human Resources department.

In this case, the teacher was given two choices: shift to working as an online teacher or resign. The teacher resigned. It set off an entire series of new responsibilities for my principal friend, from finding a qualified substitute to communicating one-on-one with students' parents about the abrupt change in their child's assigned teacher, but in the end, he was grateful. "The incident proved to me what I'd long suspected about this teacher," he said. "She was not here for the right reasons, and when things got really difficult, she resigned rather than work through it with her students."

The principal ended up finding an excellent substitute—a recent university graduate who was eager to take on the challenge of online learning—and that substitute did such an excellent job that she was hired permanently for the next school year.

## Sabotaging Leadership

Teachers with negative purpose may have a desire to disrupt those in leadership positions. Since they aren't in the job for the betterment of students, they resent the expectations or constraints leaders might put on them. It can feel like these teachers are crouched in a corner, waiting for the chance to spring up and point out—or create—problems for the principal.

My first year as an assistant principal, I encountered a teacher who jumped at any opportunity to correct my mistakes. If I sent an all-staff email, she'd shoot an immediate reply with grammar corrections, procedural clarifications, or questions that picked apart my message. In meetings, if I misspoke, she'd interrupt to correct me. One morning, as I was explaining the upcoming evaluation cycle to staff, I said, "On Monday, I'll swing by to set up an observation time." This teacher raised her hand and reminded me there was no school that coming Monday. "Tuesday, then," I said, thinking how much her comment reminded me of one a child would make. Not five minutes later, nervous and trying to focus, I made the same mistake. Before the words were even out of my mouth, her hand shot in the air. "Again. No school Monday," she said, almost gleefully. I was anxious, knowing any misstep I made would be met with a correction or question, delivered in a tone seemingly intended to undermine and embarrass me.

This teacher's behavior felt like a personal vendetta directed at me. I endured it for several months, until I finally broke down and appealed to my principal, who had heretofore honored my intent to manage the situation on my own. With his help, we called a meeting with the teacher. We spoke honestly about how her criticism seemed like public sabotage, then we outlined actionable steps that she could take to make things better.

My principal spoke firmly. "From now on, any complaints or criticisms of her"—he pointed to me—"or any issues with our procedures should be directed straight to me." In spite of my embarrassment at not being able to deal with the problem on my own, I was relieved and grateful that the principal took this stress away from me.

The new directive didn't improve the teacher's negativity, exactly—instead, she grew quietly sulky, effectively pouting her way through the rest of the school year. Fortunately, I had the support of the majority of teachers, who had recognized and been uncomfortable with the teacher's actions, and of my principal, who had identified her actions as unacceptable and helped monitor her behavior.

## Showing Disdain for Students

Teachers with a negative purpose can spread toxicity with the underhanded and disparaging comments they make about students. My first year of teaching, I worked with a man who constantly engaged in unkind and belittling conversation about students, all the time pretending he was "just joking." I found myself feeling almost queasy after spending any amount of time with him. In the lounge at lunch, he made fun of how students looked, acted, or performed. He seemed to delight in making things difficult for them. Even when interacting with students, he made jokes and innuendos veiled in humor, often leaving them bewildered. At the time, young and insecure, I didn't have the courage to call him on it, but I was shocked that he had such little faith in students. Now, of course, I understand that it was his negative purpose talking—and oh, what I wouldn't give to go back and respond appropriately.

## Engaging in Destructive Criticism

Without positive purpose to drive them, some teachers become armchair quarterbacks, criticizing every decision made by those leading the game. Their attitudes can deflate other teachers; worse, they can be contagious. Sometimes the criticism can seem harmless in small doses but becomes damaging over time—which becomes particularly evident in times of crisis.

Here's an example. Not long ago, when schools were faced with difficult questions of security after several terrifying school shootings, teachers were understandably frightened and anxious. Some, however, seemed intent on finding every loophole in security plans, perpetuating fear and making it impossible for legitimate plans to be put into place. One colleague of mine told me about staff meetings where one teacher would commandeer the entire conversation, consistently criticizing the district's evolving safety responses. This went on for months. The principal wanted to help her feel less angry and afraid, and he wanted to value her thoughts, but he also felt a need to limit her input so he could hear from others.

"I need the voices of the entire staff, not just one," he said of developing a workable safety plan. "It's mind-boggling how one teacher has the ability to derail my entire leadership process." In the end, the only relief came when his district's Board of Education adopted and implemented an official districtwide plan. "Constructive criticism is always welcome," reflected the principal, "but having a destructively critical teacher in a crisis scenario is particularly problematic because it can get in the way of productive problem solving."

# Responding to Negative Purpose

Without fail, every time I speak to a group of principals about motivating teachers, I'm asked the same question: "How do I handle my most negative teacher?" Chronically negative teachers cast such a dark shadow over a school community that principals are often at a loss as to how to intervene.

The type of negativity we're addressing here isn't the occasional frustration or criticism that teachers with positive purpose express when they think their schools are moving in directions that aren't best for students, and it surpasses the kind of negativity we all feel sometimes—maybe due to a bad day, or week, or even a really bad year. No, this is a deeper kind of negativity, a force so strong it overcomes any hope of positive change. It manifests itself in phrases like "This won't work," "This is stupid," "I'm not going to change how I do things," and "They can't make me."

How the larger teaching staff reacts to the behaviors of one extremely negative teacher speaks volumes about a school's culture. If they join in the negativity, it becomes a runaway train, impossible to stop and overtaking the entire building. If they are deflated by the negativity but lack the courage or willingness to stand up to it, teachers will become quietly dejected. But if they are willing to stand up and say, collectively, "That's not what we do here," they can succeed in squelching the negativity altogether.

Of course, it can be difficult for colleagues to stand up to negativity, especially if they suspect it will result in anger or aggression. And there's reason for them to think that way: a study on workplace aggression by Douglas and Martinko (2001) found that people with a negative affect can become aggressive toward those with whom they work. And that leaves us, as principals, flummoxed: we know that the most powerful response to negativity is collegial intervention, but we also know we can't expect positive teachers to overpower negative ones.

During the COVID-19 pandemic, a principal friend of mine chose to take on negativity about her school's approach to the crisis by cloaking everything she did in positivity. She became a one-woman cheerleading squad for the school, posting daily on social media about the good work her teachers were doing, calling teachers personally to thank them for their efforts, and making uplifting videos to send to her staff. She was crushed when one of her most negative teachers responded by posting a tweet about the principal's "toxic positivity." It took some time to talk my friend out of being truly depressed. She had learned a lesson important for all principals: you can't necessarily overcome negativity with relentless positivity. It is an example of why many principals avoid addressing issues of purpose—often, it simply seems like an impossible problem to solve.

I've done this myself. Early in my administrative career, when I was working as an assistant principal, I'd heard rumors that a particular teacher had made a paper chain to count down the days until his retirement. This would have been funny had his retirement been a week or two away, but it was several *years* away. One day, after students had been dismissed, I went to his classroom to investigate.

Sure enough, there were hundreds of tiny paper links curled around his desk, computer, phone—even his whiteboard and filing cabinets. I was appalled, and so was the principal. He tried to intervene, asking the teacher to remove the chain, but he wasn't willing to go much further, especially after the union president pointed out that there had been no contractual breach. The principal asked the teacher to at least not discuss the chain with students, though of course savvy 8th graders caught on quickly. The paper chain became a joke among students, but their parents did not find it so funny. Several of them called the school, troubled by the sense that their children's teacher was just putting in time and flaunting his disinterest in teaching.

I was certain I could talk some perspective into the teacher and convince him to take down the chain. My principal wished me well, but I could tell he didn't have hope. I went to the teacher's room during his plan period, sat down at a desk, intertwined my fingers, and took a deep breath.

"I'd like to ask you to remove the paper chain," I said. "It advertises to the students that you don't want to be here."

He glared at me. "I *don't* want to be here."

"But you are hired to teach students in a classroom in which they feel welcomed and wanted—"

"My contract requires that I be here. It doesn't require that I create a room of"—he rolled his eyes—"*rainbows* and *unicorns*."

I stared at him, trying to find words to change his mind. I made a few more attempts, but he shut me down at each effort. I fled, humiliated and discouraged, knowing he saw me as immature and naïve. I reassured myself that the students in his class were fine. They liked him, appreciated how "easy" his class was, and found humor in his "who cares?" attitude.

Were the students *really* fine? Perhaps, but they certainly weren't in the best learning environment, no matter how I might have spun it in my mind. In retrospect, I wish I'd handled this situation with more force. I comforted myself that I wasn't really authorized to fight too hard, given that I was "just" an assistant principal. I used that as an excuse, and I gave up. I'm not proud of it, and I've thought about it many times since. Having learned from my inaction, I offer here a few takeaways for principals who are up against teachers displaying negative purpose.

## Discussing Negativity Honestly

Revealing, naming, and talking about problems of purpose is extremely difficult. It often feels easier to ignore them or wait them out in the hopes the situation will resolve itself. Indeed, it sometimes does, through a retirement, transfer, or resignation. But hope isn't a strategy, and the cost of waiting for a possible resolution can be steep. It is simply unacceptable for students to have a lackluster or negative learning experience. Principals should be willing to openly discuss problems of negative purpose with teachers. It doesn't have to be a combative or aggressive conversation; it can be gentle and compassionate, an opportunity to seek mutual understanding and respect. There are a lot of ways to kindly and gracefully ask, "Do you really want to be here?" without accusation or judgment. "I know this work can be extremely challenging, and I would love to talk about how it affects you as an individual," or "None of this will be shared outside this room; I just want to understand how to make your role into one that benefits all of us—your colleagues, students, families, and you. What are your thoughts?"

Some teachers may have never truly considered their own purpose, finding themselves fully committed to a career without ever honestly reflecting on their "why." We can help them by asking questions like "What motivated you to become a teacher?" "What do you find most challenging about your job?" "Is teaching what you'd hoped it would be?" or "What, specifically, do you find fulfilling about this work?" Another approach that has worked for me is to begin by talking about expectations: "What expectations did you have of this career? How have you been 'let down' by the students, school, or profession? Tell me how it feels to come to terms with unmet expectations."

When we are courageous enough to have these conversations, they tend to end very well, especially if we avoid judgment in reacting to a teacher's honest responses. After all, mutually acknowledging a purpose deficit is the first step to overcoming it.

## Exploring Alternatives

A colleague of mine once worked with a teacher who had been struggling with her job performance. After multiple conversations in which the principal tried to build openness and trust, the teacher admitted that she really didn't enjoy working with her students anymore, and especially didn't like working with their parents. "I have to stick it out, though," she said. "I'm too far in to get out."

"But do you want to invest more years of your life into a job that makes you miserable?" replied the principal. He pointed out the satisfaction she seemed to get out of piloting new technology and fixing broken hardware and offered to help her find a different role. Just one year later, the teacher was coordinating the technology in a neighboring district. She was still a public-school employee and investing in her retirement, but no longer dealing with the aspects of teaching she'd hated. She wrote to the principal and thanked him. "By discussing purpose, you helped me find mine," she said.

I saw a similar situation unfold with a teacher who had taught freshman composition for almost 30 years, but who had grown lethargic and apathetic in the job. Her principal suggested she give middle school a try. The teacher was resistant—she claimed she wanted to retire in the exact same teaching role she'd held for almost three decades—but her principal had her involuntarily transferred to teach 8th grade English.

To the surprise of everyone involved, the teacher found renewed life and energy in her new role, even summoning up a work ethic she'd long forgotten. She enjoyed the job so much that she pushed off her retirement several extra years. It's not that she suddenly discovered a lifelong purpose that had been latent all those years; it's just that she found new energy that could sustain her for some time. An alternative teaching placement turned out to be just what she needed.

Teachers with negative purpose may benefit from moving to a different classroom or grade level or by adjusting a team dynamic. I've seen principals reassign teachers to a role more appropriate for them by changing their class assignments or content areas. I've also seen principals remove negative teachers from a team and assign them to a different team that props them up with a strong and unwavering purpose. A friend of mine recently moved a teacher from a particular teaching assignment to "break up" a duo that seemed to be languishing in a swamp of negativity together. "You know the saying. You lie down with dogs, you get fleas. Right?" he remarked with a wink. "Well, I moved that teacher away from the dogs *and* the fleas."

Providing an alternative isn't always possible, especially in small rural districts where most employees have very specific and unchanging roles. However, it's surprising how much inspiration and how many alternative options can emerge from simply asking, "Do you enjoy this work? Is it something on which you want to spend your professional lifetime? If not, what would be a good alternative?"

## Providing Appropriate Professional Development

For principals who are trying to motivate a purpose-challenged teacher, finding the right professional development with the right motivational approach can prove effective. A principal friend of mine once worked with an intervention teacher who'd had a positive purpose at the beginning of her career—at least according to evaluations from her previous principal—but had lost the energy and enthusiasm for her work. The principal planned to attend an out-of-state conference centered on how teacher teams could develop schoolwide behavior management strategies. He registered—and brought her along. "I have struggled with some of your negativity in the past," he said to her frankly, "but I'd like you to come along and be a critic of this program. When we attend sessions, think about challenges or successes that might come from implementing these strategies at our school."

The teacher soon became enamored with the energy and inspiration she experienced at the conference and grew increasingly enthusiastic about the innovative, groundbreaking teaching strategies presented there. On her return to school, the teacher had a specific role to play implementing some of the strategies she'd learned, and her renewed energy helped overcome her negativity.

## Digging for Compassion

In seeking to understand the toxic effects of negative purpose, it helps to approach with an empathetic mindset. After all, it's not easy for someone to live and work with constant negativity. As one study found, negativity is a general state that includes feelings of "nervousness, tension, and worry" as well as "such affective states as anger, scorn, revulsion, guilt, self-dissatisfaction, a sense of rejection, and, to some extent, sadness," and that it does not necessarily manifest itself through "overt stress" but tends to emerge "across time and regardless of the situation" (Watson & Clark, 1984, p. 466).

For principals, this means a teacher's negativity isn't necessarily a reflection on our leadership, our school, or our students. No matter what happens, chronically negative teachers will find something to be upset about, and they will be eager to talk about what's wrong, why it's difficult, why solutions just don't exist. It must be exhausting to be so angry, dismissive, defiant, and frustrated all the time.

I learned this lesson from a principal I met at an out-of-state workshop. Speaking to a small group, she described a particularly challenging staff member who was consistently negative, angry, and disruptive. Someone asked, "How do you manage it?" The principal smiled. "Every morning on my way to work, I dig deep, deep, deep into my soul to find my most compassionate place. I spend a little time there. I remember that my job is to be my best for this teacher, every single day." Inspired by her deliberate decision to be her best for an unhappy teacher, I promised myself that I, too, would practice digging for compassion. Over time, I have learned to find grace and space for teachers who are miserable in their work—as long as students aren't hurt in the process.

## Letting Teachers Go

As most principals know, it is very difficult to terminate teachers, even if they show poor performance, a bad attitude, and negative purpose. This is especially true in public schools with strong bargaining units or restrictive contract language. But if a teacher's negative purpose has led to negligence, a toxic environment, or identifiable damage to students, an improvement plan must be written and steps taken to remove that teacher from the school.

Empathy and compassion aside, moving toward termination is the right thing to do if it is done in defense of students. Principals need to be knowledgeable about the negotiated contract, work closely with Human Resources, document every performance issue or contract breach, and take all formal steps leading to termination. Though principals can get anxious about the subject, it is possible to have a positive parting of ways before a teacher's negative purpose leads to long-lasting damage.

Take, for example, the case of a teacher named Mia. I'd met her at a professional event for which she served as the public relations specialist. She was six months out of college with a journalism degree, and her job was to support the hosting organization with social media outreach. She was young, energetic, and endearing; I fell for her positivity, especially when she confided that she was miserable in her job. "It's just the wrong fit for my personality," she said. "I need to work with real people. I need relationships!"

When she learned I was a principal, she squealed and clapped her hands like a happy child. "I have always wanted to be a teacher," she gushed. "I think I missed my calling! I should have worked with kids!"

"It's never too late," I told her. "Many universities offer graduate programs leading to a teaching certificate." We exchanged numbers, and I encouraged her to call me if she needed anything. She hugged me. "I'm so glad I met you tonight! I feel like this is destiny!"

I felt that way, too. *She will be a wonderful teacher*, I thought. *I hope I can help her.*

I was pleased when Mia contacted me some time later to tell me she was indeed pursuing her teaching license. In the spring after she completed her student teaching, my school had an opening in her certification area. We went through the motions of the interview process, but I knew I wanted Mia to take the job. She had a fantastic interview, and the hiring committee embraced her energy and excitement just as much as I did. I offered her the job. I was so proud of her, and proud of myself, too; I felt like I'd "discovered" Mia and made a difference in her life.

The first day of school was fine. So were the second and third. The fourth day, I noticed that Mia's face was red and blotchy. The fifth day, she scowled as she walked down the hall to accompany her students to the bus, snapping unreasonably at a child who hadn't sealed his lunch box and was leaving behind a trail of drippy lunch remains.

"Are you OK?" I asked her. She shook her head and turned away. I let her go but kept an eye on her for the next two days. I was confused and surprised at her transformation from a cheerful, enthusiastic spitfire to an emotional, angry dark cloud.

At the end of the second week of school, I asked Mia to stop by my office. When she arrived, I motioned for her to sit at my small conference table, saying, "I just wanted to check on you." She sank into a chair and began to weep.

"I don't want to do this," she cried. "I hate it. I feel trapped. I thought teaching would be a great job, one where I could be creative and hang out with cute little kids all day, have my summers off and time to travel. Teaching is not me. It's not who I am."

I was stunned—and exasperated. I felt tempted to tell her to toughen up. I felt a scolding at the tip of my tongue: "You need to appreciate that you've been given the best job in the world." But I bit my lip; I knew I was looking straight at a mismatch of person and profession, and there would be no value to come from anger, from placing blame, or from wishing for a different outcome.

"Let's think about possible solutions," I said, breathing my way toward a gentle tone. Perhaps I could find her an additional mentor, give her more planning time, eliminate some of her extraneous responsibilities.

"There is only one solution. I need to quit," she blurted out. "I'm miserable. I am depressed and anxious and can't live my life like this."

Startled, I tried to slow things down. "This feels impulsive to me," I said, urging her to take a few weeks to think.

To her credit, she did all the right things. She took a short-term leave of absence, hired a therapist, and even went on medication to manage her anxiety and depression. After investing two years of her life into becoming a teacher, the unraveling wasn't simple. Her fiancé was flummoxed. Her parents, who had financed her graduate work, felt betrayed. Her colleagues were annoyed and confused. But as she "worked on herself," as she called it, she uncovered deeper issues she needed to prioritize.

In an afternoon meeting that October, Mia told me her therapist advised her to resign. She left the school that day and never returned, not even to get the personal items she'd left in her classroom. On the advice of her therapist, she wrote me a long, handwritten letter, explaining the misstep she'd taken in choosing this career path. She was also careful not to apologize. "I'm not sorry," she wrote. "I am still learning who I am." I never heard from her again.

Working through her resignation with our Human Resources department, we briefly considered our legal right to hold Mia to her contract, but we decided there was no value in forcing her to stay. I found a long-term sub to take over the classroom, communicated honestly with parents of the students in her class, and worked closely with the substitute to transition her into the classroom. Fortunately, she was a positive addition to our staff, and the students had a good school year.

I spent a lot of time wondering what had happened. In time, I've come to accept that Mia just realized, too late, that teaching wasn't right for her. And I learned, also too late, that I'd made my own mistake: I'd never stopped to think, much less ask, about Mia's *reasons* for becoming a teacher. I had really liked her fun, energetic, and sweet personality, so I'd made assumptions about her purpose. I'd thought her purpose was like *my* purpose, or like the purpose of other successful teachers I knew. But my assumptions had been all wrong. I'd been so set on having her on our team, I hadn't stopped to ask if her dream version of teaching really aligned with the reality.

Ultimately, this story has a happy ending *because* Mia walked away—and because we let her walk away. I shudder to think of the negative impact she would have had on decades of students if she had stayed in a job she hated. Schools should be full of teachers who *want* to be there. Purpose is at the root of the relationships they create and the instructional practices they master. If the root is weak, the branches will be weak as well.

We started this chapter thinking about Mr. P., a teacher who put forth minimal effort and showed little commitment to his school and his students. Although there are no magic answers for dealing with teachers like this, principals who show care and courage can find ways to navigate the most complicated situations. Above all else, the student experience needs to be a driving force when deciding how to improve a teacher's purpose.

We begin the next chapter with Miss M., a popular and effective teacher who seems to have found a good balance between her personal and professional lives. She has prioritized her teaching in ways that have a positive effect on her school and students. Then we explore the question: What can principals do to support teachers like Miss M. and ensure long-term positive outcomes for their classrooms?

# Building on Positive Priorities

*Every time you walk by Miss M.'s classroom, you can see how much students are enjoying her class. The environment is warm, welcoming, and productive. Students appreciate her timely feedback and open communication. There is a good balance of instructional methods, and she has developed an inquiry-based environment where she can provide differentiated levels of support for students. Parents are comfortable and happy with their children's emotional and academic growth. When inevitable challenges pop up, Miss M. shifts into problem-solving mode and seeks out colleagues for input and support. Miss M. feels—and shows—that she has achieved a good balance between her personal and professional lives. As a principal, you know this is a case of positive priorities in action.*

A teacher's career typically stretches over a significant span of life. There are marriages and divorces, new houses and relocations, joy and trauma and struggle. Loved ones get sick. Children are born, grow up, and move away. In that time, the teacher may go to graduate school or pursue hobbies or areas of passion after work hours. The teacher will mature, find enjoyment in ever-changing things, watch goals and dreams shift with the rise and fall of life's challenges. All the while, each August, a new roster of students will be handed out, and with that roster will come new student needs and concerns. Most teachers deal with all these challenges without pause, shifting and adjusting priorities as needed.

If purpose is the root of our motivation tree, priorities are the trunk and core. Although teachers' priorities may be understood by their teammates or close colleagues, they aren't typically as visible to students, parents, or the principal. Priorities define teachers' decisions and behaviors, which are visible to all and represented by the branches and leaves of the motivation tree.

Principals, students, parents, and even the public often expect teachers to make their jobs a primary priority. But what do we mean by setting this expectation? Do we really want teachers to exclusively prioritize their students above all else? This hardly seems fair or sustainable, but still many of us expect it—particularly if we've set the same expectation for ourselves.

I've certainly done this. In the beginning of my career as an administrator, I placed my job above all other priorities. It went well for a while, especially because, at the time, I had no partner or children. But eventually, I became overextended, tired, and resentful. I wondered what was wrong with me. I knew my purpose was positive, but I was running low on energy and enthusiasm. It took time for me to recognize that my exclusive prioritization of work was making me a weaker educator.

Many principals have experienced something similar. On a popular online principals' group I follow, principals regularly lament the lack of balance in their lives. They prioritize the needs of staff, students, and the community above everything else, and then feel deflated when no one seems to notice or care.

Just as we should not expect this of ourselves, we shouldn't expect teachers to make work their only focus. Instead, we should encourage balance and compartmentalization. Priorities don't have to be fixed or tiered. It is possible—healthy, even—to have multiple "top" priorities, particularly when we have grown skilled at managing multiple commitments by focusing on the most immediate ones. Moreover, just because teachers don't exclusively prioritize something doesn't mean they aren't doing that thing well. In other words, principals don't need to ask, or even wish, for teachers to always put their teaching first. Instead, we should support them in managing life's ups and downs and provide a secure, reassuring, and welcoming teaching environment. When teachers feel appreciated and safe, they are more likely to consider teaching to be an important and meaningful part of their lives, their identity, and their purpose, regardless of the challenges they face outside school.

# Characteristics of Positive Priorities

Many teachers have mastered the art of balancing multiple "first priorities." They may consider teaching to be a top priority while they're at school, for example, and then shift seamlessly to another priority when the school day ends. Teachers with the ability to make teaching a top priority while engaged in it are often building and acting on their deeper positive purpose, and they may have a confidence and self-assurance that make their work seem natural. They prioritize teaching simply because it's who they are and what they do. When they are actively teaching, it appears as if it's the most important thing in the universe to them. The characteristics that follow are typical of teachers with positive priorities.

## Equanimity

My friend Chelsea exemplifies a teacher with positive priorities. It is from her that I learned the word *equanimity*—now one of my favorite words, and a quality to which I am constantly aspiring. Chelsea embodies equanimity in her life, decisions, and priorities. Her classroom, too, is a place of equanimity. She is patient and calm, even when her students push and aggravate her. She is relentlessly kind. She would no more speak ill of a child, or use a sharp voice, than she would play hooky.

Many people would never guess that, in addition to teaching, Chelsea has three very young children, a small farm, and a spouse who himself works as a teacher. She is busy and her days are chock-full of responsibilities. When she is teaching, though, one would never sense how full her life is; she is never frantic or anxious. She relies on patience, kindness, and care with her students, indicating that her priority at work is to create a classroom where student learning is the goal.

Making teaching just one of several priorities is a sign of health and wellness and balance. When we leave our jobs, we should focus on the priorities of home, of self-care, of hobbies and activities that make us who we are. Taking care of yourself and your families does not mean you're not taking care of your students; it doesn't need to be one or the other. Indeed, it can—and should—be both.

## Dependability

Teachers with positive priorities can be depended on, as they are certain to follow through on their commitments. Of course, emergencies happen to everyone, and even teachers who prioritize their jobs above all else might have to make exceptions at some point along the way. But teachers with positive priorities rarely cancel at the last minute with bogus excuses. They do what they say they'll do, and they come to work with a positive attitude and stay until the end.

## Showing Up

A principal friend of mine has a science teacher on staff who has chaperoned every single high school dance for more than 20 years, and does it all with a smile. "Why do you come to every dance?" the principal asked her once. "Most teachers only volunteer to chaperone one dance a year—at the most—and usually do it *very* reluctantly."

"It's a way I can give back to the students and the school," the teacher replied. "I tell my students I'll be here, and I want them to see me being part of their important social activities just as I am part of their learning the properties of an atom." This teacher sees her role as bigger than just delivering curriculum and thinks of ways to connect with students outside as well as inside the classroom.

One teacher I know well, Amber, sticks around after student music concerts to help the custodian put the chairs away. If she's in the office and someone is wrestling with the copy machine, she'll happily stop to help. She is always the first one to offer to cover classes for a colleague when an emergency arises. Amber's habit of "showing up" makes a huge difference in her building. It is the kind of informal support that might not be captured on formal teacher evaluations yet is an invaluable contribution to the school community.

Teachers with positive priorities are available when they are needed by students, the school, or the community. They celebrate with students and colleagues during happy times and support them when things get difficult. I saw this in action during the COVID-19 shutdown in March 2020, when teachers facing their own family issues or health worries still managed to prioritize their jobs. They came together and learned how to share tips, resources, and ideas to keep our school community connected. They made movies, held a drive-by parade for students, stopped in at students' houses, designed art packages, asked questions like "How can we figure out if students have the technology they need?" Overnight, teachers expanded their repertoire to become social workers, technology coordinators, food pantry managers, and outreach experts. "It was so nice to watch teachers put their students and our school on the front burner," a colleague said to me. "I've never seen such commitment and dedication from my staff. They really showed up, and they showed up in big ways."

## Expertise

Developing expertise is a choice. Investing the required effort and dedication is something one *decides* to do. Teachers don't become experts in curriculum or instruction overnight, or even over several months; it takes time and focus over the span of a career to achieve true expertise. Teachers who prioritize their jobs and students know that they need to constantly work on instructional content, viewing mastery as a long-term goal. They are also happy to share this expertise with others because they understand that doing so is part of being a true expert.

Consider social studies teachers, who have recently had the opportunity to hone their instructional and content skills due to events in the news. In response to the growing conversation about the role of racism in U.S. history, many of these teachers have prioritized their own learning to enhance and expand their instructional toolkits and worked hard to include diverse voices in their classrooms. They have pushed themselves to grow as facilitators and conversation guides, opened their own eyes to different perspectives, and helped students to think about our world in different ways. These teachers' willingness to continuously add to their expertise reveals their dedication to their craft.

## Being Excited by New Instructional Challenges

Teachers with positive priorities are excited rather than burdened by new instructional challenges. When they find themselves teaching a new grade or class, they are invigorated by the prospect of reprioritizing their work. These teachers embrace new ways of doing things, eschewing robotic, cookie-cutter instruction for innovative and enthusiastic facilitation of learning.

## Reading Students' Records

Teachers who prioritize their relationships with students will work to get to know the whole child, taking the time to view cumulative and data files for each student. Some teachers don't prioritize this process, saying they'd rather give children a "fresh start" every year. I would argue, though, that a blind "fresh start" actually slows the process of getting to know students and disrespects the work of all the teachers who came before us. It neglects the student, too, who relies on an uninterrupted communication system between teachers for a smooth transition from year to year.

Teachers with positive priorities understand that ignoring a student's records is like reading a novel by starting in the middle.

They prefer to start on the first page: cumulative files, data reports, conversations with previous teachers, intervention and enrichment information, family history, time spent in previous schools, transiency patterns, and so on.

One teacher I know sets aside several hours each summer to dive into the special education database to read every IEP and evaluation report for each of her students. Other teachers camp out next to their students' cumulative files and flip through them all, committed to an information-gathering effort that helps them start the year off right. Being informed about student records, history, performance, challenges, and growth is an excellent example of priorities in action.

## Extracurricular Involvement

Many teachers go through cycles of after-school involvement. My husband, an athletic director, often sees teachers take on athletic coaching positions early in their careers, then step back as they settle into marriage or children or getting an advanced degree. This doesn't necessarily indicate a weakening of priorities; often it simply reflects a natural cycle of adjusting priorities to meet life changes.

When I first started teaching, I coached three sports and led two extracurricular clubs. Showing up for students was my top professional priority, and it was my top personal priority, too. I was completely committed, often putting in 60-hour weeks teaching, planning, advising, coaching, and making my classroom a place of challenge and comfort. I'm ashamed to admit that I judged midcareer teachers who didn't do likewise for what I perceived as a lack of dedication.

All it took was becoming a mother to gain humility and to shift my thinking. Working through a pregnancy, two devastating miscarriages, and another pregnancy, then managing two young children at home, I couldn't give my time to school in the same way I had before. For several years I did the best I could, but I spent every extra moment managing babies and a household. In time, I found ways to contribute by offering my skills to things I could handle during my plan period at school or at home while my babies slept. I organized an overnight field trip for about 150 students and helped manage a ticket-selling effort for an after-school play. Now, as my children enter their teen years and are developing lives and activities of their own, I give back in ways that once again involve after-school supervision, committee work, and even extracurricular activities.

My priorities shifted during the last 15 years, but never *away* from school. I have more commitments to balance, so I have learned to maximize my time and be the best person I could be at any given moment. With any luck, principals will have a mixture of early-, mid-, and late-career teachers on staff, all with varying priorities but also all aligned to the larger mission of the school. For principals to understand, accept, and ride the ebb and flow of life's cycles is a great gift to teachers and extremely helpful for creating a positive school culture.

## Engaging in Professional Development

"I'm a lifelong learner." I've heard this phrase in many interviews with early-career teachers. I always like hearing the words, but I know it will take time to determine if they will really hold true. Teachers with positive priorities understand the need for ongoing professional development and accept the time and effort that it takes. They are the teachers who provide ideas, show up with a positive attitude, and model adult learning for colleagues. Often, they will even lead professional development for others.

A few years ago, I hired a teacher who described herself as a lifelong learner. In her interview, she described her priorities as an educator, sharing her perspective that social-emotional learning (SEL) is the most important part of a teacher's mission. "We are all learning so much about SEL every day," she said. "This is my passion area. I want to be an expert on student mental health, trauma, behavior, and school response." Indeed, this teacher has continued to grow as an SEL expert and has recently been leading professional development in SEL for her peers. I won't be surprised if she is soon known at the state or national level for her work. She has made professional development a priority for herself and for others from the beginning, and many students are better for it.

## Willingness to Engage in Necessary Processes

Several years ago, our school began the process of adopting a robust Response to Intervention process. It was important, necessary, challenging work. Some teachers—particularly the most experienced ones, who had spent the early parts of their careers managing intervention needs in ways that worked for them—didn't immediately embrace the structures and protocols we'd put in place. Some struggled with the pre-scripted questions we asked of a child's learning journey. Some hated the timed, cyclical nature of check-ins with parents. Others felt overwhelmed by data entry. I knew which teachers had their priorities aligned with students and our schools' mission, though, by watching how they adapted. Even if the process seemed to slow them down, or if they felt there were unnecessary steps, they understood the bigger picture and accepted that the established system was there to help their students. As a bonus, the modeling they provided by adjusting their priorities was helpful to teachers who were reluctant to do the same.

## Thinking of Every Student's Needs

There's a great moment in the Netflix series *Virgin River* in which the character Mel asks her date, Jack, about something bothering him. He smiles and reaches for her hand. "I'd prefer to focus on what is in front of me," he says. It is a sweet, romantic moment, and I've watched it multiple times, struck by how often we *don't* focus on what is in front of us. Teachers have a million different things going on at school—distractions, commitments, competing interests. Those who prioritize teaching in the moment see what is in front of them—their students—and strive to make the classroom environment such that all students feel their learning is valued.

I know a teacher, Jeff, who makes his students feel as though they are important to him every moment they are in his classroom. When his instruction is interrupted by a visitor, or if another student asks for help, he respectfully asks for patience while he finishes his first conversation, taking care never to make a student feel dismissed. He looks students in the eye when they speak to him and is careful to listen to their intended message. He refuses to interrupt them and consciously thinks about ways to ensure each of them is seen and heard. He notices when students are detached or disengaged. He is fully present. Watching him, I am reminded of a poster my high school English teacher had above her desk: "Be Where You Are When You're There," it said. I thought a lot about that poster back then, and I continue to think about it today, especially when I see teachers prioritizing the students in front of them.

## Accepting That "Life Happens"

The older I get, the more easily I accept that I cannot control what will happen in the future. Planning is certainly a strategy, but ultimately, I have to adapt when I'm thrown a curveball. Teachers who prioritize teaching are able to cope and carry on when there are challenges to their plans.

A sudden case of the flu, a fender bender on the way to work, an ill parent or spouse—none of these should disrupt a classroom full of students. On the contrary, teachers should know such things are inevitable and have emergency plans in place for substitute teachers. We all know it's not healthy to agonize over potential problems or disruptions. But that's different from accepting that they are inevitable and having a plan in place to keep the learning going.

# Supporting Teachers with Positive Priorities

The entire school community benefits when teachers prioritize excellent teaching even in the face of distractions or roadblocks. To that end, here are some ways principals can help teachers with positive priorities keep them that way regardless of any external challenges they may encounter.

## Providing Empathy, Sympathy, and Trust

It's been quite some time since I was the parent of infants, but I do remember the bone-deep exhaustion that came with that role. Some days I felt like I was just going through the motions, trying to manage work and life and pumping and breastfeeding and three, four, five wake-ups a night. There were times my eyes were so tired they literally ached. I can't even remember entire chunks of my professional life during those times. In another period of my life, when my grandfather took his own life and our family scrambled to make sense of what he'd left behind, I could not even begin to think of work in any meaningful way. During these times, my supervisors were kind, gracious, forgiving, and helpful. Had I been unfortunate enough to have a principal who didn't understand life's curveballs, who didn't know how it sometimes came to a screeching halt, I would have had to contend with too many additional worries, anxieties, and self-questioning cycles. Principals build loyalty and gratitude with teachers by supporting them through difficult times. Empathy, sympathy, and trust are all tools for us to use when teachers have to reshuffle their priorities.

Of course, we can't completely relate to every possible circumstance. I am lucky to still have both my parents, for instance, and can't imagine how it will feel when they pass away; they anchor me and remind me who I am. But I imagine the pain that comes with such a loss is deep and devastating, so when teachers experience the death of a parent, I trust them to take the time they need to honor their loss. I trust they will deprioritize school to prioritize themselves. This is true with other life events as well. Even if I can't personally understand or relate, I have faith that a teacher may need to reshuffle their priorities, and that all will be fine in the end. I can show sensitivity and care without having had the exact same experiences myself.

## Eliminating Priorities That Don't Support Student Growth

A friend of mine remembers her first few years of teaching, when she had difficulty differentiating among her priorities. "Everything seemed crucially important. *Everything*," she said. "I made everything school-related a priority and spent an exorbitant amount of time trying to please my students, my principal, my teammates, and my students' parents." Her principal noticed that she was working herself into anxiety-provoked knots and offered some good advice.

"Public education is full of distractions, mandates, and requirements," he told her. "Everyone thinks *their* thing is the most important. The only thing that really matters, though, is the experience we provide for students." He helped her to think about things that were bogging her down, encouraged her to work with a coach to make her grading practices more efficient, and asked that she reevaluate and adjust how she organized her time at school.

One of my goals as a principal is to help teachers remove superfluous priorities—or better said, remove *barriers* to prioritizing students. I cancel staff meetings if they aren't essential, put updates into only one weekly email, avoid trying to guilt staff into attending events not related to their work, and try to delegate or eliminate administrative tasks for them whenever possible. I budget money for resources and supplies that make their jobs easier. Principals can help teachers simply by removing anything that takes time or energy away from students.

## Noticing, Complimenting, and Reinforcing

When teachers show they can manage and adjust priorities to maximize the student experience, a principal's acknowledgment can help validate and reinforce their work. Principals should actively seek to compliment teachers both formally and informally. I try to follow this mantra: "If you think you're showing enough appreciation, you're probably halfway there." If a principal sees evidence of a teacher's solid, consistent planning; a schedule or data-collection system that gives frequent and applicable information to students or parents; an enviable organization of priorities—well, it is wise to commend them. Hearing them, seeing them, and showing up with compliments and validation—the way we want teachers to show up for their students—reinforce the efforts they are making to prioritize their work.

## Seeking to Understand

It is easy to think we know our teachers well, especially if we have worked with them for a long time. In truth, we only know what they tell or show us. We should never assume we have a full understanding of their school and life responsibilities, or that we know all the priorities they may be juggling at any given time. As someone once told me, "You never know what is happening behind someone's front door." She meant this as a call for empathy. But not knowing what is behind that front door doesn't mean we shouldn't knock and ask, "How are you doing?" If we aren't invited inside, that's fine—but at least we extended a hand. As a principal, it's always better to ask than to assume.

Admittedly, it can be overwhelming to worry about other people's lives and priorities. When I am feeling stretched thin, the last thing I want to do is muster up the energy and enthusiasm to check in on people. In fact, a reluctance to ask often indicates that my own priorities are out of whack. But you know what fixes the situation immediately? Just doing it. I can seek out teachers and take a moment to ask them questions like these:

- How are things going for you?
- Are you facing any new challenges with students or parents?
- Are you feeling confident about your teaching?
- How is your family (or your pets or hobbies)?
- What do you need?
- How can I help?
- It's a tough time of year. I know I'm struggling to stay on top of things. How are you doing at handling it all?

Beyond invigorating me and helping me recommit to my own professional priorities, checking in on teachers helps me know what's happening with them, makes me qualified to reassure them if they feel unbalanced, and gives me the opportunity to offer them support and understanding.

## Listening Closely to Teacher Feedback

We all hate it when we don't feel heard by our supervisors. I once had a boss who looked over my head when I spoke, as if he couldn't wait for me to be finished because whatever was behind or above me was so interesting. It drove me crazy. When teachers tell us things, they want us to listen. Sometimes they want action;

other times, they just want to be heard. As Maya Angelou famously advised, "When people show you who they are, believe them—the first time." When teachers show you what they need, either through words or through action, it bears taking time to listen and respond.

## Being Proactive

Principals can proactively support teachers by anticipating any upcoming challenges they may face and guiding them through them. "When the baby comes," you might say to an expectant mother, "don't even think about returning to work until you've taken time to recover and spend all the time you can with the baby." To a parent whose child has just graduated, you might say, "I know your son is leaving for college in the fall. I hope you'll feel comfortable taking personal days to enjoy this important transition with him." Or to a teacher who is also becoming a graduate student: "You're teaching new content next year, and I know you're also taking graduate classes. What can I do to help you manage your busy schedule?" Acknowledging upcoming challenges will, above all else, send the message to your staff that you prioritize them just as you want them to prioritize students.

We opened this chapter by thinking about Miss M., who had established a system built on positive priorities to create a warm, welcoming, and calm classroom environment. Unfortunately, it's a lot less fun to try to support teachers who do not, cannot, or will not make teaching one of their life's priorities. In the next chapter, we will consider negative priorities and ways principals might intervene to help teachers who exhibit them get back on the right track.

# 5

# Addressing Negative Priorities

*Ms. C. has always been a strong teacher. As her principal,*
*you've always liked her very much, both personally and pro-*
*fessionally. She is kind, patient, and organized. Lately, though,*
*you've heard some of her colleagues complain about her, and*
*even had a parent email you to complain about the length of*
*time it takes Ms. C. to respond to student work. You start pay-*
*ing closer attention and notice that Ms. C. seems to be taking*
*shortcuts—her planning seems haphazard, she is distracted*
*and harried, and she has been keeping to herself rather than*
*contributing to her team.*

*Knowing you should check in with her, you invite her to*
*swing by your office after school. She seems annoyed and*
*hurried when she arrives. It's awkward at first, but when you*
*tell her you've been worried and want to know if she's OK,*
*she takes a seat and reaches for the tissues. She tells you her*

*partner has taken a transfer to another city, and they are trying*
*to decide if she and their children will join him or if he will*
*continue to commute back and forth. She is coming to terms*
*with her choices—either being primarily a single mother and*
*living where she has a good job and family support, or moving*
*to a new city with her partner, where she would have no job*
*and no support.*

*Listening to her quandary, you know that Ms. C.'s decline in*
*performance is a matter of priorities. In this case, hers have*
*been forced to change.*

In teachers who typically display positive priorities, performance problems will quickly attract a principal's attention. Such teachers may suddenly and unexpectedly be unavailable when needed, retreat from some of their responsibilities, or disengage from colleagues by closing their doors during common planning or work times. Or they may seem distracted, as if they have removed themselves emotionally from the student experience.

This is when a principal needs to ask, "Is this teacher struggling with a problem of purpose, priorities, or patterns?" As a principal, I have struggled with this question. I even struggled with it when I was a teacher myself. It's easy to judge others who don't prioritize their work as I would. Over time, I've learned that I cannot align my own priorities with anyone else's. I can never fully understand why other people make decisions as they do, what forces are pressuring them, or what structures their choices.

Twenty-five years ago, when I was a novice teacher, I worked on a team with a veteran teacher—we'll call her Susana—who had been transferred to our building from another school. Susana and our principal, Mr. K., seemed to be professional confidants; he stopped by most mornings to talk with her, closing the door behind him. I didn't know much about Susana, but from my outsider's view, her priorities seemed out of whack. She was late to school every day, missed almost all staff meetings, skipped out on important professional development, and raced to leave school as soon as the buses had left the parking lot. Her lesson planning was uninspired, as her students seemed to spend a lot of time silently reading, writing, or completing worksheet packets. She missed a lot of school.

Susana had positive traits, to be sure—she was funny, charming, and always kind, so her students didn't seem affected by her detachment. In fact, I found myself annoyed at how much they seemed to genuinely like her, despite her frazzled and haphazard approach. While I spent hours upon hours responding to student work, I didn't feel she was giving students meaningful or timely feedback on their papers—in fact, there were times when she wasn't grading student work at all. She had a breezy attitude, laughing her way through blunders as if none of them mattered. "I'm such a mess," she'd say. "I can't believe you all put up with me."

The four members of our team reluctantly picked up the slack when Susana didn't do her share of the work. She thanked us often, but we would dismiss her, empowered to meanness by a shared annoyance. I'm ashamed to admit we often whispered and gossiped about her. How could she care so little about her students? Why wasn't she working as hard as we were? Wasn't she ashamed to be so disengaged? We couldn't believe Mr. K. didn't address Susana's apathy directly and were confused that the opposite seemed to be happening. He seemed to look the other way, giving Susana breaks he wouldn't—I assumed—give to anyone else.

Later that year, I got a serious, career-changing lesson in humility. It was late spring, and the year was wrapping up. At the end of a team meeting, Susana said she had something she wanted to tell us.

"The only person who knows about this is Mr. K.," she said. "He knew I didn't want to become an object of gossip, and I'm glad he honored my secret. But now I'd like to tell you what has been happening in my life." Just one day earlier, she had finalized a divorce from an abusive spouse and had been granted full custody and a hard-won restraining order. She'd lost her home, was estranged from her beloved in-laws, and had just moved into temporary housing with her three teenage sons. Outlining the upheaval in her life during the previous two years, she described it as an ongoing hell she wouldn't wish on her worst enemy. "And I know this has been very difficult on all of you," she said. "Thank you for sticking with me."

I felt hot with shame. We were all silent.

"Is there anything we can do?" one of our teammates finally asked.

"No, not really," said Susana. "I'm just glad I have this job so I can support my family on my own. Mr. K.'s support has been amazing and saw me through this painful time. We are all lucky to work for someone like him. He has a humanity that doesn't always exist in school leadership."

That day I learned two things. First, we can never know the weight others are carrying, so passing judgment on how they prioritize their work is unfair at best, ignorant at worst. I made a pledge to do better. Second, I learned how a skilled principal can guide someone through hard times. Susana's life priorities had been upended, and our principal's flexibility and patience were the gifts she needed to carry on. He had honored Susana's private story, checked in on her often, cut her a break, recognized her strengths, and had faith that things would work out in the end.

And they did. As Susana's life settled down, she showed that she was an excellent teacher with an ability to inspire students as readers, writers, and thinkers. In fact, a few years later, she took on the role of instructional coach for our district, which showcased her own patience and kindness in working with others.

I saw Susana not too long ago. Almost 20 years had passed since we worked together, but she looked like she hadn't aged a bit. Her cheerful demeanor filled the air in the room. She told me about her contented life on her little horse farm, the visits she enjoyed from her sons and grandsons, and her new marriage to a loving, supportive partner. She was planning for retirement and spoke excitedly about her next life chapter.

After talking a while, I said, "I feel like I owe you an apology." I stumbled my way through a heartfelt and regretful explanation of my own personal reflection and what I'd learned from making assumptions about her when she'd been dealing with a personal crisis.

She smiled and hugged me warmly. "Grace is a gift," she said. "I have been given grace, not only from Mr. K., but from many people. My goal is to just give it back." Moved, I promised to do the same.

The principal was the real hero of Susana's story. He hadn't confused priorities with purpose by assuming that Susana's purpose had turned negative. Instead, he recognized that she was facing unexpected and unmanageable life challenges and simply needed support getting through a difficult time.

In cases like Susana's, it is entirely possible that priorities don't need to be addressed at all; a principal just needs to offer patience, time, and support. Teachers admire and respect principals who can tell when a soft and empathetic hand is the only intervention needed.

In other cases, a principal may need to set straightforward expectations—especially if a teacher's problems with priorities are negatively affecting students. Sometimes teachers grow too comfortable and start taking lazy shortcuts, or they're distracted by other commitments, or they become disengaged to the point of negligence. In these cases, a teacher's priorities may need a little boost—and who better to provide that boost than the principal?

# Characteristics of Negative Priorities

Negative priorities often manifest themselves in behaviors that are atypical of the teacher, who may have previously exhibited both positive purpose and positive priorities—connecting well with students, being inspired by the art and science of teaching, and having strong relationships with the school community. At some point, the teacher may have grown distracted and overwhelmed and started to express frustration, stress, or exhaustion, particularly with things that hadn't previously been an issue. In this section, we will discuss some of the evidence indicating that a teacher's priorities have shifted away from school and consider some examples of situations that might cause the teacher to perform differently.

## Detachment

A few years ago, I spoke with a principal who was frustrated with a teacher who had withdrawn from regular school activity. She wasn't a traditional classroom teacher; instead, she served in a support role, working with small groups of students who needed intervention services.

"I don't know what's going on with this teacher," the principal said. "She calls off sick on important PD days, doesn't attend staff meetings, and doesn't read my email updates. And because she isn't there for big events, she misses smaller ones." For example, the school had hosted a special assembly, and she stayed in her office rather than come enjoy the experience with the students. She stopped participating in safety drills. She had even begun leaving school early without reporting it to the principal.

"Perhaps she has too many things to keep track of, or feels the information is never relevant, or maybe she has simply stopped caring," the principal theorized. He knew his communication system was not a problem, as other staff members were using it successfully, so he set out to determine why the teacher was deprioritizing his communication—and to consider solutions to fix the problem.

The principal had a meeting with the teacher, who reassured him that his communication strategies were effective and efficient; the problem was that she had begun feeling detached from the school. She explained that her office—a small room at the very end of the school's longest hallway—kept her isolated and disconnected. It was dark with no natural light, and none of her colleagues made their way down the hall to say hello.

"There are entire days I don't talk to another adult," she said. "I don't feel a part of the school, and I haven't made it a priority to come out and connect with others."

They struck a deal: she'd reprioritize her commitment to stay connected and informed, and he'd try to find a different office placement for the next year. Before long, the teacher was back in the mix with her colleagues and staying informed about new initiatives and developments.

## Annoyance and Irritation

When teachers feel annoyed with a student or irritated about a mandate, or when they dismiss a job requirement or ignore a parent question, it may be because there is something else they'd rather be doing—or need to be doing.

I once worked with a teacher who, in an about-face from her typically patient and calm personality, went through a stretch when she seemed to snap at everyone. Once, after I greeted her cheerily in the hall after a long weekend, she grumped, "Three-day weekends aren't so great." Her tone took me aback, and I must have looked stunned. She apologized immediately. "My husband told me I need to stop being like this," she said. I went to her room at lunch to check in on her, and she confided that she was struggling with an empty house since her youngest son had gone off to college. "Packing up his room was the *worst*," she said. She grew emotional as she explained that she hadn't been able to think about anything else since.

"Everything is irritating me lately," she confessed. "Since my kids are gone, it seems like it doesn't matter. Nothing matters." Hearing herself explain her feelings, she acknowledged that her pain was affecting her priorities. She had a therapist she saw regularly. "It might be time to double my sessions," she said, ruefully. "I need a reminder to care for myself and my own needs." Her irritation at things that had never bothered her previously indicated a negative shift in priorities.

## Feeling Overwhelmed

We've all had times when we've had so much to juggle in our personal lives that our work seems like just one more thing on a long to-do list. With time, organization, and support, most teachers can come out of these challenges professionally intact, with their students no worse for wear. Other times, though, they need a principal's help.

I was discussing this with a colleague of mine recently, and he told me about a teacher on his staff who couldn't keep up with her grading. She had just returned to work after having twins. A high school English teacher, she'd always prided herself on giving detailed feedback on student writing.

She'd come to the principal in tears. The babies weren't sleeping; her husband was traveling a lot; she was exhausted. "She needed a mental break and time to catch up," said the principal. "I hired a substitute to team-teach with her for a few weeks while she got a grip on her grading. Then, I paired her up with an instructional coach who gave her some ideas on how to be more efficient with her grading practices."

Although life events are often out of our control, sometimes being overwhelmed is self-inflicted. I once had a very difficult conversation with a teacher who had taken on a role as a salesperson for a multilevel marketing company that sold expensive jewelry. She was very proud and vocal about her "side hustle," as she called it. Over time, the side hustle seemed to become her main hustle. I suspected she was spending her plan period, lunch period, and even class time managing her sales. Parents, students, and colleagues reported that she had deprioritized teaching to the point of negligence.

I met with this teacher and shared my concern. When I recommended that she tend to her business after school hours, she insisted that she never worked on the business at school. Knowing this wasn't the truth, I asked if she was using school resources—time, technology, contacts—to promote her business. "Doing so would be a breach of your contract," I pointed out.

She backtracked quickly. "No, no, no," she said. "I'm just overwhelmed. My student caseload is very difficult this year, and I'm trying to update my curriculum wiki—" She stopped, having quickly run out of excuses.

"I suspect you are overwhelmed because you're trying to do two different jobs," I said. "But while you are here, you need to prioritize your students."

She made an angry exit, but later, several staff members thanked me for identifying a problem—and calling the teacher on it.

## Communicating Poorly with Parents

The traditions and expectations parents hold about teacher communication vary from community to community. In some schools, parents expect frequent and ongoing communication from teachers;

in others, parents don't engage much at all, and teachers struggle to get them to respond to any outreach efforts. But teachers have a responsibility to try to connect with parents, regardless of the expectations; when they don't, or if they stop trying, this may indicate negative priorities.

## Disinterest in Professional Development

We have all had the experience of participating in professional development that didn't feel applicable to our work, so we can understand the frustration teachers feel when sitting through PD they don't believe is relevant to them. That said, in general, teachers with positive priorities understand the value of ongoing learning and will seek it out, recognizing that there is always something to gain from an educational training—so resistance may indicate a shift in priorities. Sometimes teachers won't attend professional development sessions at all, or they will attend only when they are required to or if they need contact hours to renew their license. Other times, if given a choice in learning opportunities, they may choose only the easiest option that requires the least amount of accountability.

## Avoidance

Sometimes teachers whose priorities have turned negative will shift their focus away from job requirements that are, admittedly, challenging or not particularly enjoyable. They may avoid adopting new technology, completing required training, engaging in the evaluation process, or completing small but consequential tasks.

# Responding to Negative Priorities

When a teacher is derailed by life's challenges, prioritizing school can be impossible—and it is part of our job as principals to help teachers navigate these difficult circumstances.

I am still heartbroken when I think about a teacher I knew who went through a period of seemingly insurmountable challenges. After several months of trying to remotely manage care for her ill mother, she made the difficult decision to resign from her teaching job, moving across the country to provide personal care. Soon after settling there, she secured another teaching job, but it seemed doomed from day one. She was not confident or comfortable in her new school, she struggled to make friends and build relationships, and she had a hard time grappling with the emotional and physical toll of watching her mother's life come to an end. Although she had always struggled with disordered drinking, alcohol began to take over her life.

One day, her principal found her with her head on her desk, passed out. Upon recognizing she was drunk at school, he immediately suspended her until the termination process could begin. In a devastating blow, her district also petitioned the state's education department to have her license revoked.

Ashamed, lost, scared, friendless, and alone with her dying mother, the teacher emailed me. "It's no wonder I lost my job," she wrote. "It was the last thing I was thinking about. Addiction made me unfit to teach." Still, she felt hurt by how quickly and aggressively the district cut her out and eliminated her career. "I lost everything," she said. In a step of extreme courage and grace, she entered an extensive rehabilitation program and began to learn more about her addictive behaviors and how they were symptoms of deep depression and anxiety. Her wayward priorities hadn't even been a conscious decision; her life had scrambled her priorities out of her control, leaving virtually no support system to help her.

I believe all teachers can be helped and supported, and that it's especially necessary when they are dealing with extreme personal crises. With that in mind, let's consider ways we can step in to help teachers before wayward priorities do damage to a teacher's purpose, patterns, or career path.

## Providing Temporary Flexibility and Resources

When my teacher friend lost her job and career, she understood why, but she will always mourn the loss of her teaching certificate. She wishes her principal or district had provided a connection to an employee assistance program (EAP) or given her time to seek treatment during her suspension. Perhaps she could have begun a process of recovery *and* maintained her identity as a teacher.

These days, most districts do have some sort of EAP to help teachers during difficult times. We can easily guide struggling staff members toward this resource, which is typically confidential and free to the employee. We don't even need to know why or how their lives might be challenged to connect them with professional help that might alleviate some of the pressure they feel.

Usually, if a teacher's priorities have shifted out of balance, some school-based interventions or support can help. Not long ago, a principal I know made an offer to a teacher whose wife was traveling internationally for several weeks. Her temporary absence had left this teacher alone to care for four young children, one of whom had significant special needs. He needed to leave school midday to check on the child while the home health aide took a lunch break. The principal not only approved of the teacher's regular midday absence, but also offered additional help at school. "I will find coverage for your study center, and I will personally cover your bus duty for the next few weeks," she told him.

"I can't let you do that," the teacher said. "It never goes over well with colleagues when someone gets out of duties. They think it's unfair. They might judge me for shirking my responsibilities."

The principal acknowledged this truth, but pointed out, "Since they are your friends, they really should understand. And if they are irritated that you're 'getting out of something,' they are just as likely to be irritated if you overextend yourself." The teacher laughed, seeing that either choice might result in collegial irritation. He accepted the principal's offer and spent the extra time he'd been given catching up with his responsibilities.

It's a wonderful thing when a principal develops a reputation among staff as someone who understands life's curveballs and is willing to jump in and relieve pressure when needed.

## Expressing Empathy

In the hustle of running an entire school, principals can sometimes forget to call upon empathy when teachers struggle to prioritize their teaching responsibilities. The capacity to truly place oneself in the position of another is tested during these times, but principals who do so will reap the benefits of loyalty and gratitude from teachers.

Empathy goes beyond thinking "I feel really bad for that teacher." It's deeper and more personal: "If I were in that teacher's position, how would I be feeling? How would I manage my workload? How would I reconcile all the things I need to do to manage my life?" Usually, answering these questions reveals an important truth: that teachers truly are doing the best they can in an impossible situation.

## Shifting Job Responsibilities

Principals who know when and how a teacher's priorities have been challenged can proactively consider changes that will help carry those teachers through the difficult time until they get back on track.

I once worked with a teacher who had been raised on a farm several hours from where he now lived and taught. His parents were aging and none of their children were able to take over the farm, so the land was put up for sale. It was an emotionally and physically exhausting time for this teacher. He drove four hours "home" every weekend to help his parents prepare for auction, all the while mourning the loss of his childhood home.

In the two months leading up to the auction, and for several weeks afterward, I was able to adjust this teacher's schedule so he could leave work a couple hours early on Fridays, giving him a head start on his drive, in exchange for taking over an extracurricular supervision duty on Wednesday nights. The change was only temporary, but I was committed to making it work because I had faith that this teacher's priorities would soon shift back to his regular teaching schedule. The flexibility paid off, and then some—to this day, the teacher expresses gratitude for the support that helped him get through a difficult time.

## Modeling Solution-Based Problem Solving

I learned a great strategy not long ago that I find hugely helpful: whenever a problem comes across my desk, I encourage those involved to come up with at least two possible solutions for it. I try to make it a challenge: "Let's see if we can do a 'two-for-one,'" I'll say. My request usually triggers more than just two solutions, providing multiple options for us to consider. Some of them are unreasonable or even outlandish, but there are usually some good nuggets to consider, and the process usually triggers even more ideas. The right solution might involve a change in job assignment, an adjustment of duties or schedules, temporary relief from responsibilities, or even—and it's a legitimate option—quitting the job altogether.

I recently spoke with a teacher about possible changes to her home life that could alleviate stress at work. She was stretched thin each morning, always late and frazzled before school began. She said she spent every morning racing frantically back and forth across town to get her kids to two different day-care facilities. One child went to a kindergarten enrichment program, and the other to a toddler preschool program.

"Let's think of two solutions to this one problem," I said. "What can you do differently? Anything goes. Let's list every single option."

"Well, there are some options that I'm not willing to do," she protested.

I smiled at her. "Those sometimes lead to the best final choice," I replied.

We made a list. She could put her children in the same day care, but that would dramatically increase her monthly cost. She could take a leave of absence until her children were older. She could ask her husband to shift his work hours so he could help with transportation. She could hire an in-home sitter.

Each of those ideas had some sort of hitch, but they helped us come up with another idea altogether: posting on Nextdoor to ask if any neighbors would be willing to be paid to transport her children to day care. She posted her request, and somebody answered: a retired nurse who lived a few streets away. After a few weeks of acclimation, during which we temporarily adjusted the teacher's work hours to allow for flexibility and a later arrival, the teacher felt confident that the neighbor was more than capable of providing the emotional support her children needed at the beginning of each day. In the end, considering multiple solutions to our one problem led us neatly to a positive resolution.

## Encouraging Support Systems at School

Many of the priority challenges discussed in this chapter originate at home, but work stressors can also have a big impact on teachers' home lives. Work and home are often tightly intertwined for educators. A bad day at school carries over to home, and a bad night at home carries into school. Just as teachers' home and work lives often overlap, so, too, should their support systems—and a school community can be a fabulous support system for teachers. Colleagues can become close friends and confidants, experiencing life's ups and downs together. They celebrate positive things, like weddings and new babies and graduations, and when there is illness and death, they make casseroles, organize meal trains, and hire housecleaning services. Principals should be proud when their staff members come together to both celebrate good things and lift one another when things aren't going well. They can also be part of these efforts, leading a culture of group support, mutual understanding, compassion, and reciprocity. That's when a school really begins to thrive.

Principals who understand that teachers' priorities will ebb and flow over the course of a career, and who flex their expectations with a teacher's needs, generally receive respect and appreciation from their teachers. I often think of Susana's comment about receiving and giving grace. Grace is always the best choice when a teacher is struggling with priorities. A principal's support, guidance, and understanding can make a difference as to whether a teacher will work through the issues and "come back," better than ever, or whether the wayward priorities will lead them too far astray.

In the next two chapters, we will discuss the third and last element of our metaphorical motivation tree: professional patterns, which, like the leaves of a tree, are the most visible of the three motivational categories to students, colleagues, and community. Patterns can be the admirable traits that define a strong teacher—or the problematic habits of weak teachers. As we did with purpose and priorities, we will examine the characteristics of positive and negative patterns and explore ways for principals to support the former and disrupt the latter.

# 6

## Building on Positive Patterns

*As a principal, you open each school year with a staff meeting. Among other things—fun icebreakers, curricular overviews, updates on district information—you take time to review your staff handbook, which covers your standard professional expectations of your staff. As you do, you make eye contact with a teacher near the front of the room. Mr. G. may well have written the handbook himself. He is always on time, always well prepared, and supports the school's mission with his actions, communication, and student-centered decision making.*

*Mr. G. takes his job seriously, rarely missing work unless he is ill or has an unavoidable commitment. When he is absent, his substitute plans are detailed and easy to implement. He always dresses professionally, gets along well with colleagues, and avoids negative behaviors such as gossiping or spreading misinformation. He keeps himself informed, cheerfully attends meetings, and keeps up-to-date with professional development. Looking at him in the meeting, you realize you never, ever worry or wonder about his performance. He is a prime example of positive patterns at work.*

Teachers who are regularly responsible, reliable, and responsive have typically developed a system of positive patterns—the habits and routines of day-to-day conduct. These teachers embody the best professional version of themselves and serve as an important role model for colleagues and students. Teacher patterns are rooted in teachers' purpose and supported by their priorities, but can also benefit from a principal's guidance.

Teacher contracts outline positive patterns in the form of professional expectations, such as the minimum minutes a teacher will be at work, how much planning time they will receive, how much sick and personal time is allotted, and specific processes for disciplinary action if teachers don't adhere to these expectations. For schools without unions or negotiated contracts, these expectations might be more fluid and up to a principal's discretion. Ideally, everyone on staff understands the value of having these expectations in place, and a principal's role is simply to monitor patterns and intervene if a teacher needs guidance. However, I have known principals who have never read their teachers' contracts, leaving them ignorant about explicit contractual expectations. When principal expectations are not aligned to those spelled out in teacher contracts, conflicts arise, people take sides, and someone—a union president, a central office expert—will need to step in to provide clarity and direction. Often, the principal will "lose," especially if the contract language clearly contradicts something the principal has asked a teacher to do. Moreover, principals can quickly get themselves in trouble if they discipline a teacher for failing to do something that isn't contractually required. Principals should know the district expectations before establishing school-based protocols for teachers to follow. When expectations are aligned, teachers can settle into the patterns that will define their daily work.

Teacher patterns are visible to everyone in a school community and directly impact teachers' reputations. What's more, when students know teachers have set high standards for themselves, they are more willing to meet high standards as well. Students who see that their teachers are on time, respond to questions quickly and with care, and work hard to provide high-quality resources for instruction can recognize the value in their own timeliness, responses, and work ethic. It is a cyclical and self-fulfilling process of betterment.

# Characteristics of Positive Patterns

Because positive patterns are so visible, principals can find ample evidence of them by paying close attention to simple day-to-day interactions teachers have with others. Principals can stop in for classroom visits, observe classroom management patterns, keep an eye on how teachers communicate with parents, and monitor student progress.

An absence of complaints from colleagues, students, and parents may also indicate that teachers are displaying positive patterns. There are many teachers in my building who go years and years without a single parent raising a concern. These are the teachers who always seem to get it right: they are proactive communicators, they anticipate student needs before issues arise, and they respond to problems responsibly and with care. Year after year, students declare them their favorites, and parents speak of how grateful they are.

Hundreds and hundreds of successful student experiences stack up in the wake of teachers with positive patterns. These deeply entrenched habits can help define a school, so let's take some time here to examine some common examples.

## Respecting Protocol

I appreciate when teachers understand that some school matters are nonnegotiable if a school is to be run well. Although I try not to micromanage the professionals on my staff, I expect them to meet the following requirements:

- Maintaining dependable and reliable attendance
- Adhering to safety standards
- Following required safety drills
- Creating a secure, comfortable learning environment
- Arriving to assigned duties on time
- Taking and recording student attendance accurately
- Updating grades and assignments in the learning management system
- Writing required reports, such as IEPs and evaluation team reports, carefully and on deadline
- Reading district and building emails for updates
- Attending staff meetings
- Following the discipline-referral process, pushing back only if teachers feel strongly that it isn't serving students or have constructive feedback on how to improve it
- Updating Response to Intervention plans with accurate and applicable data
- Preparing for and executing parent-teacher conferences
- Bringing up concerns, criticisms, or suggestions for improvement in respectful, productive ways

These are just a few of the myriad standards principals may have for teachers. When teachers exhibit positive patterns, principals don't need to follow up with reminders or punitive action. They will never need to ask questions like "Have you managed to finish . . . ?" or "Did you receive the communication about . . . ?" or "Are you aware that you need to . . . ?" For teachers with positive patterns, the answer to these questions will always be yes.

## Thorough and Consistent Instructional Planning

There is a debate among principals about the need to collect lesson plans from teachers. Years ago, it was standard for principals to require that teachers turn in a copy of their instructional plans every single week. Many required these plans to follow a standard template with fields for objectives, materials, actions, assessment, and outcomes. Some principals read the plans intently, even "marking them up" to offer feedback and suggestions for the teachers.

This expectation used to be so ingrained that it would have been unthinkable to reconsider it. Although some teachers grumbled about the weekly task, others welcomed the chance to show off their organization and planning. From the perspective of principals, it was a way to monitor classroom instruction and keep an eye on the teacher's curricular intentions—or, at least, provide the illusion they were doing so.

Many principals no longer require teachers to turn in plans, recognizing that plans do not necessarily indicate excellence in teaching. After all, anyone can make plans appear thorough and rigorous, and recent shifts to online and asynchronous resources make the previous practice of attaching student worksheets to the plans moot. As principals have moved away from this requirement, a system of trust has developed, built on an assumption that teachers can and will complete planning on their own. Many principals have recognized the need to respect the professionalism and skill of their staff. In some cases, a principal can request a lesson plan or justification of instruction if needed, but most principals don't require *every* teacher to turn in plans *every* week. This is a good thing. If we expect teachers to differentiate their instruction to meet individual student needs or adjust lessons based on student response and understanding, we cannot ask them to plan instruction days or weeks in advance.

Teachers with positive patterns have never needed to be required to turn in lesson plans to motivate them to stay on track. They plan because they want to be ready for their students, not because they want to meet an administrative requirement. They know and monitor their curricular expectations and fit each day's content activities to the needs of students. If their principal says, "Tell me about today's instruction," these teachers can provide a rationale for the day's objectives, explain what materials or resources will be used, demonstrate how progress will be monitored, and identify the intended outcomes. They can also explain what they will do if students don't grasp the content and how they will support students who need further challenge. These teachers tie together prior content and a "bigger picture" of future learning, always keeping an eye on the scope and sequence of their entire year—consistently, without complaint, and without ever doubting the value of planning.

## Providing Student Choice, Student Voice, and Evidence of Learning

Not long ago, I presented at a conference for school leaders about the impact a teacher's positive patterns can have on a school. "I get what you're saying about patterns," a principal asked. "But what is some evidence I can look for when I do a walkthrough of a classroom? I want to know how a teacher's patterns directly influence a student's academic growth."

"Let's stop there for a bit," I said. "Think of your strongest teacher. The one you never worry about. The one who seems to have mastered the art of teaching. What does that teacher's classroom look like?"

The principal described the classroom of a language arts teacher in his building: "Well, there are books organized by genre and reading level. There are areas in the room where student work is displayed, and she has set up a technology station in which students can peruse the websites created by other students."

"What are the classroom routines?"

"She starts each day with conversation, just catching up with the students and saying hello. But then she gets their input on the previous day's learning, asking students if anything confused them. She reviews notes or online resources from concepts leading up to the day's work."

"What else stands out to you about her classroom?"

"There is a lot of project-based learning. Students get to choose how they show their knowledge by deciding what they care about and applying it to the real world."

This principal's description points to three important components in the classroom, all of which could be attributed to positive patterns: student choice, student voice, and readily visible examples of student learning. "Well, there's your evidence," I said. "This is a teacher with positive patterns. The student learning experience is solid based on these observations."

## Connecting with Students

Strong teachers make it a part of their daily routine to connect with students. I work with a teacher, Ms. K., who walks her students to the bus every single day even though she isn't required to do so; there are plenty of staff on bus duty. She does it anyway. As her students exit the building, she says goodbye and something personally applicable to each student: "I can't wait to hear about your birthday dinner," or "Good luck in your Fortnite tournament tonight," or "Make sure you ask your mom what she thinks of your new book."

I asked Ms. K. once, "Why do you walk your students to the buses every single day?" She looked at me like I was crazy. "I love sending them off with a special goodbye that tells them I'm excited about tomorrow." I raised an eyebrow. "Well, OK, I don't always love doing it, especially on days like this," she said, gesturing to the icy rain falling outside. "But it's just a habit. I do it the first few days of school and I just never stop."

Ms. K. offers just one example of the countless ways teachers connect with students. I know another teacher who makes it a habit to attend at least one artistic, athletic, or extracurricular event throughout the year so his students see his support outside the classroom. Another teacher uses dialogue journals to conduct written conversations with her students. There are no specific "correct" or "incorrect" ways to connect with students; the important thing is that it is done.

I'm reminded of the day before I started teaching, almost a quarter-century ago, when I became suddenly anxious that I had no idea how to be a teacher. My father listened as I fretted and then told me, "Listen. The one thing that students really want is to be able to talk. About themselves, about life, about you, about one another. Make it a habit to start each class by letting the students talk, and maintain that habit throughout the year. That's all you need to do." It was great advice.

## Responding to Assessment Data

Another habit of strong teachers is ongoing monitoring of student progress. Strong teachers keep an eye on formative and standardized assessments, watching for an upward trajectory and accounting for occasional outliers. They communicate student progress to parents and use it to justify instructional decisions. They value data as a tool for monitoring student growth.

These teachers also assess the progress of each class as a whole. They might see that most students in a class were unable to show understanding of a particular concept, for example, indicating a need to revisit it. They also compare class data with overall school data, asking questions like "Is there something missing in my classroom?" and "What are my classroom's areas of strength?"

Not long ago, a multilingual learner moved to the United States and settled in our district. The student's initial assessment data were extremely concerning, indicating huge gaps in language skills. Fortunately, the teacher didn't panic, choosing instead to commit time to getting to know the student. After just a couple of weeks, the teacher discovered that the student had strong verbal communication skills, an enthusiastic work ethic, and strong writing abilities when given enough time to think and process the language required. Such a detailed evaluation could never be—and, in this student's case, had not been—captured in a 45-minute standardized assessment.

"This student will benefit from the gift of time," the teacher told me. "I am keeping an eye on assessment data, but I also want to work on some of the school skills not captured by that data. I'm confident she'll be caught up to her peers in just a year or two." This wide-angle view of assessment data indicates that the teacher had taken the time to pull together multiple measures for the student— which in turn points to the teacher having positive instructional patterns in place.

## Differentiating Instruction

We know that students need different levels of support at different times, and teachers with positive patterns seem to provide such differentiated support naturally. After getting to know students as learners, they monitor formative assessment data and adjust the pace and practice for individual students. Although it was once a confusing concept to grasp and implement, differentiation is now a resting state for teachers with positive patterns.

## Pursuing Innovation

It may seem paradoxical to suggest that the pursuit of innovation is characteristic of teachers with positive patterns. After all, innovation is a disruption of patterns, no? It can be—or it can be its own positive pattern.

One teacher I know commits herself to learning at least one new technology tool every single summer. She enrolls in an online technology forum, sets a goal, and takes it upon herself to learn new software that she can use in her classroom. Teachers who make new learning a habit tend not to fall behind and are less likely to be negatively affected by outdated instructional practices.

## Providing Timely Feedback

Few things are more frustrating for students and parents than a teacher who does not provide timely feedback. Students want to know how they've done. When a teacher takes too long to respond to student work, gives minimal score-based grades, or misses opportunities to provide constructive feedback, students lose any enthusiasm they may have to do their best.

Of course, meaningful feedback takes a long time. My first year of teaching, I had 135 students on my roster. As an enthusiastic English teacher committed to having students write, write, and write some more, I spent virtually all my free time, including evenings and weekends, reading and responding to student writing. I knew this wasn't sustainable, but I was committed and wanted to make feedback a prominent part of my work with students.

In talking with other teachers in my department, I discovered I wasn't alone. We all wanted to provide timely and helpful feedback to our students, but we were spending too much time doing it. So, we came together and worked toward an efficient groove with our grading practices. We streamlined some of our assignments. We learned how to incorporate conferring and peer support into our work. And we decided to make Fridays a fun challenge: we would stay at work until everything was graded, then go out to dinner to celebrate the start of a grading-free weekend. On Mondays, all our students knew they would have feedback to start off a new week.

After we had established this tradition, our principal said she heard from parents how appreciative students were to have a feedback timeline they could count on. "As a department, you've turned feedback into a dependable routine," she told us. It was the first time I realized that providing regular, consistent student feedback could be considered a habit. Teachers with positive patterns make feedback a constant loop and a nonnegotiable part of their work.

## Communicating with Parents

A principal friend of mine once told me about two teachers in his middle school who were complete opposites when it came to communicating with parents. One teacher had terrible communication habits, believing that her students were "capable of keeping track of their own learning" without input from her. She never sent emails to parents, didn't develop any sort of newsletter, and didn't update the online grading system until the very end of the term when grades were due. She never sent positive notes home to parents or discussed classroom management issues with them.

Her colleague across the hall was the opposite. She shared with parents a Google Sites page that provided a rough summary of her teaching intentions for each week as well as links for practice at home. Some parents used the site and others didn't, but it didn't really matter to the teacher; she put the information out into the universe for them to use if they liked but didn't judge or pressure them if they didn't.

"Why do you think these two teachers are so different in their approach to communication?" my friend asked me. "The first teacher has a strong purpose and definitely prioritizes her work. She just doesn't take the time to communicate with parents. The other teacher seems to do it without even thinking about it."

"I think it's just a habit," I said. "If the first teacher can get into a rhythm like the second teacher, she can quickly establish positive communication patterns. She can even team up with the other teacher to streamline their communication."

I've worked in schools where parents ask a lot of questions and expect thorough, accurate, and regular communication from teachers. I've also worked in schools where parents don't worry at all about the goings-on in the classroom; they trust teachers completely and don't need or depend on a teacher's communication. Regardless of parent expectations, teacher patterns should include regular efforts to keep parents up-to-date about what's going on in their children's classroom.

## Being On Time

Teachers who are always late to school tend to chip at the morale of teachers who are never late. Although it would be easy to accuse a perpetually late teacher of negative purpose or priorities, more often, it is a case of negative patterns.

I once worked with a psychologist who was late to every single evaluation team conference—a meeting she was required to host and lead. It drove me crazy; all her meetings felt awkward and disorganized. I tried to be patient but finally decided to speak to her about the problem. She admitted it was a real concern and explained that her mornings were full of chaos and challenge. She was divorced, and her young children stayed with her on school nights. Her daughter had diagnosed autism that manifested itself in tantrums, refusal, and defiance. Her son, irritated by his sister, engaged in passive resistance by ignoring morning expectations; he stayed in bed far too long, took ages to get dressed and ready, and then invariably forgot something he needed for school. The children seemed to take turns making a huge mess that needed cleaning up before one of the three dogs made it worse. They often missed the bus, so she had to drive them to school. "Every morning is a disaster," she said. "I can't even think about school until I'm walking through the door." Though this was an example of misplaced priorities, I suggested that developing new patterns might help the teacher to become more punctual. She agreed to meet with her ex-husband and explain the difficulties she was facing. To her surprise, he offered to come by in the mornings to help out. With time and practice, the two established a new routine for getting her children situated in the mornings so she could get to work on time. Finally, her team no longer had to sit awkwardly until she arrived to start morning meetings.

### Deflecting Stress

Stress is a very real concern for educators. There are deep stressors, such as student safety and behavior management issues, that can impact a teacher's purpose and priorities. There are also lower-stakes stressors, often occurring daily, that threaten teachers' patterns—and those of their colleagues, too. Teachers who feel anxious, unprepared, late, or out of the loop may carry stress on their shoulders in a way that creates stress for students and other teachers. By contrast, teachers who have settled into positive patterns are stress deflectors. "It'll be OK," they say. "No problem. We'll figure it out." Through their calm confidence, these teachers help those around them to feel less stressed as well.

The difference between stress creators and stress deflectors is evident during moments of uncertainty like power outages or technology failures. Teachers with positive patterns are usually prepared for these kinds of scenarios, so they don't miss a beat when facing them. They simply maintain their routines, making small tweaks to keep things rolling, without transferring anxiety or stress onto others. With positive patterns in place, unexpected stressors don't feel like such a big deal.

# Supporting Teachers with Positive Patterns

As we've seen, teachers with positive patterns make a principal's job easier in many respects. Because patterns are so visible to others, they are the yardstick by which parents, colleagues, and the community measure teachers'—and schools'—success. By following the guidelines below, principals can help ensure that teachers embrace a system of patterns that benefits everyone.

## Establishing Expectations

At the start of this chapter, we discussed how a failure to communicate expectations can lead to confusion or frustration. Principals can't presume that expectations will be met if they don't first outline what those expectations are. Some principals create expectations in a collaborative way, such as calling a leadership team together in a workshop to set expectations that matter to them as a group. If the staff is small, this might be a great idea; the principal can facilitate as the group determines what patterns denote excellence for teachers and should be adopted. If such a workshop isn't feasible, or such an activity might cause tension and conflict, principals can just communicate what patterns they value in writing to individuals, groups, or the whole staff. At my school, we rely heavily on a staff handbook that documents expectations about safety protocols, instructional and planning practices, professional dress and timeliness, and assessment timelines and reporting. The handbook also includes guidelines for various procedures. Staff read it on their own, and it helps us all to have a reference in our toolkit.

## Frequently and Immediately Acknowledging Positive Patterns

Principals can easily point out positive patterns as part of their ongoing conversations with teachers. I try to do this by directly tying my acknowledgments to the expectations I have previously communicated, as in these examples:

- "I can tell you have read and honor the teacher handbook! You do a great job meeting and exceeding our staff expectations."
- "I appreciate that you value timeliness."
- "Thank you for always having your paperwork in on time."
- "Your students can consistently count on you to greet them at the door, cheerful and ready for the day."

- "Your room is always clean and orderly and provides a calm environment for learning."
- "I hear so many compliments about the organization you bring to parent-teacher conferences."
- "Your energy and enthusiasm for planning engaging lessons is outstanding."

Recognizing the little things helps honor the countless ways teachers establish positive patterns.

## Ditching Rigid Accountability Measures

When teachers are following positive patterns that benefit the school, principals can reward their efforts by exempting them from oversight they do not need.

I once spoke with a principal who asked all teachers to log their arrival on a sign-in sheet in the office every morning. It was a requirement started by the principal before him, but he thought it seemed like a good way to hold teachers accountable, so he kept it up—even though, by his own admission, his teachers were remarkably punctual. I challenged him on his thinking.

"This is an outdated—and, I would argue, insulting—procedure that could easily be removed," I said. "You probably think your teachers are punctual because of the sign-in sheet, which certainly encourages people to come in on time. But if you remove the sheet, you remove the extrinsic motivator and reinforce the intrinsic motivator. Teachers will come to work on time because they want to, or because it's the right thing to do. In fact, it's likely they will even begin coming in early."

I noted that the sign-in system might be causing teachers to hurry in the mornings, breaking speed limits and screeching into the parking lot just so they can sign the sheet in time. "But they are doing good work," I said. "Why not reward them by removing the culture of anxiety?"

He agreed to try it. Not long after removing the sheet, he was proud to report there was no difference in teacher arrival times;

everyone was still on time or even early. "And they seem less grumpy in the mornings," he laughed. Success!

Another principal I know asked teachers to formally write down and share their professional goals with her at the beginning of every school year. After a few years, she recognized that this was a waste of time for the many teachers who consistently displayed positive patterns in their daily work, so she removed the requirement. She still meets individually with teachers each year, but she now uses that time to informally discuss teachers' professional goals, including what they hope to accomplish throughout the year and how they intend to measure their success.

There are many other ways for principals to reward positive patterns. Intervention specialists who always have impeccable IEPs could be exempt from having to turn them in ahead of time for review, for example, or teachers who always schedule, plan, and complete parent-teacher conferences might not be required to turn in conference sheets. Teachers who consistently meet expectations around routines, protocol, policies, and procedures shouldn't be expected to report their every action or engage in busy work.

## Monitoring Teacher Satisfaction

I prefer to proactively support teachers rather than to react when things go wrong, so I try to engage them in ongoing conversation about their work satisfaction. Once a year, I formalize these conversations by sending a survey out asking staff if they are happy in their current role or if they would like to change subject areas or grade levels. Many of my colleagues do something similar, such as scheduling biannual meetings with staff just to check in and see how things are going. These kinds of overtures give principals a good idea of how satisfied teachers are in their jobs, how confident they are in their content knowledge and instructional skills, and whether they are interested in a change to help them remain the best professional version of themselves.

≈ ⫶ ≈

Principals have the power and responsibility to honor and support teachers who exhibit positive patterns, and the payoff is well worth it: our schools flourish when they are staffed by teachers who consistently bring their best professional selves to school. In the next chapter, we'll examine what happens when teachers fall into bad habits and routines, and we will explore ways principals can quickly and effectively intervene to make things better.

# 7

## Addressing Negative Patterns

*Ms. S. is an extrovert with a magnetic personality. Students, parents, and colleagues all seem to adore her; she is able to talk to anyone, anytime, anywhere, about anything. She lingers by the staff mailboxes, next to the coffee pot, in the lounge after lunch, after her required lunch duty. All that talking has become a pattern and makes her prone to being late—to her classes, to her assigned duties, to important meetings. She is always apologetic, rushing in with a cheerful excuse such as "I am so sorry! I got lost in conversation!" But getting lost in conversation makes her miss some of the basic requirements of her job. Although she is well liked, her colleagues get frustrated because her inability to monitor her time leaves them to pick up her responsibilities. A simple conversation is needed to address her negative pattern of tardiness.*

Negative patterns are the small but impactful behaviors that have an immediate effect on teachers' colleagues and students. Working alongside someone with negative habits will frustrate, flummox, and possibly infuriate those who are left to pick up the slack. Fortunately, teacher patterns are not necessarily permanent and can be improved with support from a colleague or principal.

On the surface, negative patterns seem like no big deal—like they could be fixed with just a little bit of effort or self-awareness on the part of the teacher. Often, though, teachers are completely unaware of the impact their negative patterns have on others. If not dealt with, these patterns can not only disrupt student learning but also breed resentment among colleagues. Following are some common characteristics of negative patterns that principals would do well to notice and address.

# Characteristics of Negative Patterns

Rarely do teachers start a career with negative patterns; instead, they tend to fall into them over time. These can be a direct result of negative purpose or priorities, but they can also be manifestations of boredom, stress, or laziness. If principals notice teachers' negative behaviors repeating themselves—not once, not twice, but enough times that they become a pattern—it is worth considering an intervention. In this chapter, we will focus on patterns that can be easily improved by an open, honest conversation or a simple review of expectations.

## Excessive Complaining

We all have times when the daily frustrations of life and work get to us and we feel the need to complain. But complaining can become a habit. I've watched this phenomenon over the course of my career, and it's one of the most deflating human tendencies to observe. Someone begins to see the glass as half-empty, then proceeds to complain and complain and complain about the glass as though it is *completely* empty. No matter how well things are going or how many positive people surround them, some teachers fall into a rut of constantly grumbling about how hard things are.

## Neglecting Colleagues

Healthy schools have staff members who watch out for one another. This spirit of collegiality is hard to quantify, but staff can sense it: teachers willingly cover one another's classes if a colleague needs to leave school early, they split up and share planning and preparation tasks, they help one another out without question, they show up in times of difficulty and crisis. That spirit is what I treasure most about my current school: I believe there is nothing the staff wouldn't do to step up and lend a helping hand to someone else. In that way, we are like a family, full of love and respect and internal support.

As in many families, though, some people give more than others. Teachers who are always willing to help others out with class coverage—for a restroom break, say, or a quick visit to the lounge for more coffee—will begin to feel stretched thin and disregarded if their colleagues start to exploit that generosity by taking longer or more frequent breaks. Teachers in these situations can become resentful and frustrated before they even realize it.

## Managing Time Poorly

Being late or habitually forgetful may be indicators of wayward time management. Teachers will occasionally develop patterns of committing too much time to one thing to the detriment of other things. Those who manage their time poorly—who lack the planning, foresight, and discipline to get things done in spite of being completely capable to do so—are exhibiting a negative pattern of behavior.

## Carrying Stress

In the previous chapter, we discussed the difference between stress creators and stress deflectors. There's a place in the middle, too: stress carriers. For our purposes here, I'm referring specifically to those who carry low-stakes stressors, not the deeper ones that can threaten a teacher's purpose and priorities. Low-stakes stress carriers tend to perseverate on every tiny little thing that bothers them throughout the day—and they like sharing that stress with others by commiserating with them. Teachers can carry stress without even knowing that they're doing it—they are simply in a constant state of anxiety and worry.

Years ago, I worked with a teacher, Mr. A., who shared a classroom with another teacher, Mr. S., whose job responsibilities included helping students prepare for the SAT. Mr. A. spent a lot of time listening to Mr. S. talk about the stress of his job. What if students didn't do well on the SAT? What would happen to their chances of being accepted to college, of attending a school of their choice, of landing a good job after graduating? Mr. A. empathized with the stress of Mr. S.'s work and, over time, began to absorb it. After a while, he, too, began to fret about the SAT.

When I recognized that Mr. A. was spiraling, I went to speak with him about it. He was able to acknowledge that the stress he felt was not *his* stress. "I know the administration of the SAT actually has no impact on my job responsibilities," he said, "but it still bothers me." I told him I believed that absorbing other people's stress is a habit that can be broken. Together, we brainstormed ways he could relieve himself of this stress that wasn't his to carry.

## Poor Planning

A principal friend of mine told me about a teacher who joked about her "495 plans." The teacher had fallen out of the habit of planning her lessons at school, preferring instead to socialize with colleagues or leave school to run errands during her preparation period. She "planned" her lessons each morning as she sat in traffic on Interstate 495 on her way to school. The principal observed that those lessons reflected her poor planning—they felt rushed, frantic, disorganized. "It's a terrible habit she's developed," the principal told me. "She is an experienced teacher, so she thinks she can do her job with limited planning. But the bare minimum isn't working. I need her to dedicate some specific time to preparing for her students' learning." Planning poorly on a regular basis is a negative pattern requiring a nudge and a reminder of expectations.

## Neglecting the Classroom Environment

Not long ago, I was driving through the town where a friend of mine, a kindergarten teacher, lived. I called her on a whim.

I'd known her since elementary school, but we hadn't seen one another in years. It was Saturday afternoon, and she happened to be in her classroom, catching up on some work. "Come see me!" she squealed—so I did. She gave me directions to her school, I picked up coffee and some cookies, and she met me at the door. The first thing she did after we exchanged hugs was apologize for some of the bulletin boards in her room. "I don't think I've changed them in five years," she admitted. "Maybe more. Maybe almost 10 years." She looked sheepish. "I think my principal hates me."

"Your principal can't hate you," I said. "I bet your principal loves you. And look—here you are, working on a Saturday afternoon."

"Yeah, but I just fell out of the routine of updating my classroom," she confessed. "I used to give it a fresh start every year. But it's so much work. So tedious. And I ran out of new ideas." She looked at me. "Be honest. As a principal, do you care about bulletin boards?"

"I'm not going to answer that question!" I laughed. "I'm your friend, not your evaluator."

"But I really want to know," she said. "What do you think? I won't take it personally. I promise."

I chose my words carefully. "While I don't believe updated bulletin boards mean a teacher is 'good' or 'bad,' I do believe that updating them shows updated *thinking*. I love it when teachers keep their classroom fresh and new, because then their students will think of the room as fresh and new, a welcoming place created just for them."

She nodded, glumly. "I figured."

"Hey, let's do it. Together. Now," I said. "I have a few hours until I have to hit the road again." She grinned. We found the roll paper, talked through some themes, and caught up as we cut, snipped, and stapled.

"I'll keep up on it," she promised as we hugged goodbye. "Come back next year. You won't recognize the place."

## Disinterest in the Roots of Discipline Problems

Some teachers fall into a pattern of removing discipline problems from the classroom without trying to get to the root of them first. Not long ago, a principal friend of mine worked with a teacher who had started referring discipline problems to the office after years of never doing so at all. Many times, he felt her referrals were unsubstantiated. He watched this pattern play out for quite some time before finally bringing it up with the teacher.

"Do you think this is a particularly difficult group of students?" he asked.

"No," she said.

"Have you contacted individual parents when their children are struggling with behaviors?"

Again, "No."

"Have you considered a positive behavior support classroom system?"

"No."

As the teacher listened to her own answers, she came to admit that she'd gotten lax when it came to behavior management. The conversation served as the nudge she needed to rethink her approach.

## Not Providing Feedback to Students

Even teachers who value feedback may occasionally fall behind on providing it to students to focus on more pressing instructional requirements. But when this becomes a habit, students lack the information they need to improve as learners. Parents of students who struggle with grades are often the first to point out the problem—which is usually when the principal gets involved. "There are assignments listed in the grading system, but it's weeks after the due date and there is no feedback," parents might say. "It's hard to keep track and hard to help my child if we don't have baseline information about performance."

## Responding Poorly to Challenges

All teachers face small disruptions or challenges throughout their school day that don't necessarily constitute a crisis but still serve as minor annoyances that need to be dealt with. Teachers with negative patterns may not be equipped to handle them with calm or ease. If the day doesn't go as planned—there's an unexpected fire drill, a drop-in evaluation from the principal, an email from a frustrated parent, a request to cover a colleague's class—teachers without positive habits in place may feel off-kilter when confronted by such challenges and appear unable to adapt or respond appropriately.

I once worked with a teacher who was constantly misplacing her keys and phone. It happened at least twice a week. Each time it happened, even though she knew that the items were somewhere in the building, she was unable to get back on track until they were found. She would leave her students unattended while she poked her head in others' classrooms, disrupting students and teachers throughout the school to ask if anyone had seen her keys. It was a bad habit that had a negative effect on many students, and I found myself worrying about her students and the impact on our school culture.

## Addressing Negative Patterns

Negative patterns can usually be disrupted with a quick intervention. Social correction from colleagues is the most effective kind, but since teachers work so closely together and will often absorb the implications of a colleague's habits or routines, it often falls upon a principal to address the issue. This can feel ridiculous, especially when reminding a teacher about the most basic of expectations.

"Sometimes I feel like I'm just a babysitter of adults," a colleague of mine complained after having to remind a teacher of the school's procedures for checking materials out of the library. "It's just like reminding them to do their chores and clean up after themselves." Fortunately, it's not completely like babysitting, because teachers usually do know exactly what they are supposed to do; they just got lax or distracted, and a quick reminder will often be enough to set them back on track.

For some reason, principals often get nervous about addressing these small breaks in positive patterns. We often hope the problem will fix itself or just go away. We want to be liked, we don't like conflict, we don't want to get into an argument, and we certainly don't want to have a showdown of power. For these reasons, simple conversations about patterns can make principals even more anxious than conversations about bigger issues of purpose or priorities.

But actually, these conversations shouldn't cause stress, especially if the principal-teacher relationship is strong. Respect begets respect; when a principal quickly and honestly addresses negative patterns without resorting to punitive action or making the issue bigger than it is, there is a strong chance the teacher will make an immediate and positive change. Here, then, are guidelines principals can use to have these kinds of conversations—beginning with one of my most strongly held beliefs about leadership.

## Going Directly to the Problem

Back in high school, I was a proud member of the track team. It was a great experience, except for the extra sprints we had to do if anyone on the team was late for practice. And someone—usually the same someone—was always late. The intent, of course, was for the team to pressure the latecomers into valuing timeliness; suffering together through those extra sprints would bring us closer as a team. Except it didn't. Those of us who were always on time grew resentful and frustrated, and the one or two athletes who were frequently late didn't seem to notice this brewing discontent. All year long, the wrong people were punished, and it led to zero changes.

If nothing else in this book resonates with readers, I hope the importance of directly addressing the specific problem at hand does. Too many principals address the specific problems of one or two teachers by reprimanding the whole staff. I did this myself when I first started as an administrator. If one teacher was not helping to keep the teacher workroom clean, I would send an email to everyone saying, "We all need to come together to ensure our shared space is clean." If two teachers were habitually late, I would tell the entire staff about the importance of timeliness. If three teachers missed a deadline, I would remind everyone about the importance of the deadlines. I have come to think this is one of the biggest mistakes principals can make. Sending group reprimands creates paranoia—"Is she talking about me?"—which leads innocent staff to feel wrongly accused. This approach divides a staff, increases anxiety, and rarely resonates with the intended audience anyway.

Teachers have much more respect for principals who *go directly to the problem to solve it*. If you're not sure who the problem is, it's better to try to find out—watch, listen, ask questions—rather than scold the whole group.

## Starting with a Conversation

Principals often avoid conversations about patterns, especially if the problem seems inconsequential. "I felt like acknowledging it made it more of a 'thing' than it needed to be," a colleague told me about addressing a teacher who was completing his IEP plans late. In this principal's home state, IEPs were required to be emailed to parents five days before the official IEP meeting, but the teacher had been habitually turning them in just one or two days ahead of the deadline. "His plans are always well written, and parents don't seem to mind," the principal told me. "If I address this, I feel like I'm being petty."

"It just takes one parent, or one problem with the IEP, to call attention to this problem," I responded. "If that happens, you'll have a hard time defending the teacher. Especially because you know, right now, that the problem exists. Why wait? Just talk with him. Tell him what you've noticed. If he's the diligent and responsible teacher you think he is, he'll tighten up his deadlines and you won't have to worry about it any longer."

"Maybe I'll just send him an email," the principal said.

"Email can be perceived as a cop-out," I said. Many of us prefer email because we hate to walk into a conflict, and email feels less risky than speaking face-to-face. But conversations like this shouldn't be confrontational. "Think of it as a nudge, a reminder, a callback to what he already knows he should be doing. He'll respect you for bringing it to his attention." Besides, I said, conversations aren't misunderstood as much as emails can be. And they can't be forwarded.

The principal agreed. Later, she told me that the teacher had acknowledged that he'd gotten lax about his deadlines and cheerfully promised to do better. "The conversation took all of 30 seconds," she said. "I was so worried I was overreacting—which, of course, was an overreaction. Addressing it made it as small and fixable as it had always been."

## Being Honest and Taking Ownership

When teachers have positive purpose and priorities, a lapse in patterns does not need to indicate anything bigger than it is and should be discussed in clear and honest terms: "I've noticed . . .'"; "I just wanted to remind you . . .'"; "Can I suggest . . . ?" Too many principals let their nervousness or their wish to be liked prevent clear, honest, open conversations. They are afraid to just address a problem head-on. Again, it's far easier to just do it than to cloak it in complicated explanations or long-winded half-truths.

Principals should never try to deflect responsibility from the real issue or, worse, from themselves. "This isn't something that bothers *me*, but a few of your team members have complained," for example, or "Several colleagues have come to me about this issue, and I thought you would want to know." This is an instant culture killer that pits team members against each other. If the negative pattern bothers you, own it. If it doesn't bother you, don't address it.

## Getting to the "Why"

Getting to the "why" is a great way to begin conversations with teachers about difficult patterns. For example, say a teacher is struggling to keep up with inputting grades in an online grading program. Is the teacher feeling overwhelmed? Is the teacher creating too many graded assignments? Does the teacher not see value in grades as a communication tool? Is the process taking too long to complete? Finding and focusing on the core reason behind the problem will help the teacher and principal come together to solve it.

## Providing Additional Training and Resources

Some teachers fall into negative patterns owing to a lack of necessary knowledge or training. Take the example of the teacher who isn't inputting grades on time. Perhaps he doesn't know how to efficiently use the system, so the process is particularly time intensive for him. A quick session with a technology coach might fix the problem right up.

I once worked with a principal whose teachers were reluctant to adopt a new technology platform that allowed for instant updating, saving, and sharing of documents. These teachers were trying to use materials they had developed several years earlier on now-obsolete technology. They were used to the old way, they said, and didn't want to learn something new. Their principal finally insisted they evolve to the updated system, providing them with two days of release time to complete online training and convert their resources to the new system. Despite initial reluctance, the teachers soon saw the value of the new system and were grateful for the knowledge that helped them develop new patterns.

## Reviewing Expectations

When teachers aren't meeting expectations, a simple reminder is often all that's necessary to correct the problem. "I just wanted to remind you that our monthly staff meeting begins right at 8 a.m.," you might say, respectfully, to a teacher who has come in late repeatedly. Or, to another teacher: "Having your door unlocked promptly after lunch allows students to get in the room and prepare for class." If a teacher has started to wear clothes not aligned to your district policy, you can say, "I just wanted to remind you of our district's professional dress expectations." If teachers become defensive when you offer these kinds of reminders, resist the urge to respond with defensiveness of your own. Reviewing expectations is just that—restating facts to someone who may have forgotten them. Facts aren't feelings, so they shouldn't get complicated as feelings often do. I try to avoid mixing up the two, sticking just to facts when I need a simple problem to be fixed.

## Distinguishing Between Negative Patterns and Mere Annoyances

Just because something irritates you doesn't mean it is a negative pattern. As principals, we want to advocate for our students and teachers, but it's impossible to have a school environment with no irritants or distractions. Principals should only focus on teacher behaviors that go against their contracts or school policy, not smaller things that might irritate or bother us personally.

I had a teacher call me once in tears after a conversation with her principal. She explained that when she was not teaching, she was involved in an intense training program for competitive weight-lifting, which meant she had an extremely strict diet. Each day, she used her midmorning plan period to peel several hard-boiled eggs and eat them with a bag of microwaved spinach. Her principal was annoyed. "The entire lounge smells like cooked spinach," he told her, asking that she not use her plan period to eat that "foul food."

"Well, he can't tell you not to eat particular foods," I said. "If your meal schedule is getting in the way of your students' experience, then yes, he might have a case for input on the timing. Otherwise, I think you can eat your spinach and eggs." She decided to try to speak to him again, hoping to come to a mutual respect about her nutritional needs and reassure him that her meals would not interfere with her teaching. In the end, they reached a solid solution: if she prepared the food at home and simply warmed it up at school, the odor wasn't as strong, and she actually saved a few minutes of time. Both the principal and the teacher benefited from the compromise.

## Sharing Leadership (to a Point)

Empowering teachers to make leadership decisions helps them feel invested in success. A teacher I know was recently asked to be part of a team that would plan and organize her school's professional development. Her principal had noticed that she seemed apathetic about the school's professional development plan. "I had been showing up late to PD, not really engaging in the learning," she admitted. "He knew that if he put me in a position to make decisions about the PD, I would be more invested in its success." It worked. For several years, she served on the committee and then served as a cochair, helping construct the vision for the entire school.

There are limits to this approach, though. Principals who share too many leadership responsibilities with teachers may have a negative effect on those teachers' lives, as making critical school-wide decisions can actually decrease motivation and increase job stress (Davis & Wilson, 2000). Why might this be? Perhaps asking a teacher to take on additional responsibilities makes them vulnerable to conflict when their colleagues or peers disagree with their decisions or input. Further, it can lead to a competitive culture if leadership isn't distributed in a fair and reasonable way, creating a perception of favoritism. The key for principals is knowing each teacher's strengths, asking for input, and letting teachers openly share what they want or need to improve. If everyone has a chance to step in and lead, and if decision making is shared equally among staff, it can be a positive solution for the entire staff.

## Abiding by the Five *R*s

You may have heard of the "five rights" followed by medical professionals when they administer medication: they check for the "right patient, right drug, right dose, right route, and right time" before proceeding. I have a similar set of guidelines for thinking about staff: teachers in the right place in the right rooms doing the right thing (for them!) in the right way means they are doing the right thing for students. If a teacher's habits indicate there is a problem with any of these, a principal and teacher might come together to consider changes. Habits are reinforced by the situations in which we develop them, and we want those situations to be as "right" as they can be.

## Encouraging Teamwork, Collegiality, and Communication

"A rising tide lifts all boats." I once worked with a superintendent who loved this adage, with good reason. She believed every teacher had something unique and important to contribute to a team, and she knew that teams are more effective when everyone works toward betterment together. When one person establishes and implements a system of positive patterns, it sets an example for all others—and when someone on a team develops negative patterns, it can be helpful for the whole team to provide support for improvement. Negative patterns can fester when teachers are isolated, but they can quickly be corrected by the positive influence of helpful, purpose-driven colleagues.

Over time, I have come to recognize that social connection and social correction are quite similar. If teachers have a strong connection with their colleagues, they become accountable to them and will be more likely to understand the impact negative patterns have on a team. As a result, they will be more likely to self-correct their negative patterns and work to be the best versions of themselves. They will enjoy being one another's emotional and professional support and will be able to communicate issues with one another more effectively.

## Encouraging Confidence and Efficacy

Getting caught in a cycle of negative habits may chip away at teachers' confidence and sense of efficacy, leading them to stop believing in their own ability to be excellent. Principals who want to help teachers break negative patterns might remind them of the specific strengths, skills, and knowledge they possess and point out how negative patterns are affecting their potential.

## Coming Up with Solutions

I truly enjoy trying out unconventional solutions to problems. Sometimes the answer is so simple it's hard to believe in retrospect that it wasn't obvious all along. When I had an overly chatty teacher who habitually showed up late, for example, a frank conversation and an Apple Watch with vibrating reminders solved the problem.

The teacher who always lost her keys? Her team bought her a Tile for Christmas. Done.

Remember the teacher who "planned" lessons in traffic on the way to work? A reshuffling of her routine was able to get her back on track. In speaking with her, the principal had said, "Tell me how you use your plan period."

"I need to call my mother and check in with her," the teacher said. "She's elderly and needs the routine of my check-in. My plan period is the perfect time to do it."

"What if you call your mother every day on your way to work, and then use your planning period to prepare the next day's lessons?"

The teacher stared at him for a long time, and he didn't know if she was angry or just taken aback. "Well. I guess that would work," she said slowly. And just like that, her planning improved.

"I don't know if she really flipped her planning with her daily phone commitment," the principal told me later. "What I *do* know is that she recognized the reality of the problem by hearing suggestions for solutions. It made her change *something*, and the result was better instruction for the students. That's really all I needed."

## Choosing Your Battles

Wise principals pick their battles and learn the beauty of letting things go. During the COVID-19 pandemic, many of us perfected this art, because things that had previously seemed very important became the last things we were worried about. Being on time to work? Not a concern; we were more worried about who could even *come* to work. Updated grades in the system? Not a worry; we needed to make sure students had technology. There were so many differing perspectives on what should be done, how things should be handled, and what school should look like. For a long time, I let many things go, realizing that some of the negative behaviors were symptoms of teachers' fright, anxiety, or trouble balancing personal and professional expectations. As long as students had a positive, welcoming, safe learning environment, I didn't much worry about a lot of other things. Deciding whether to take on a battle or let it go depends on the situation, the setting, the teacher, and the likely outcome. In the end, the biggest barometer, for me, is this: will choosing this battle improve the school experience for students? If so, I'll take it on. If not, it might be better to pick something else to worry about.

Negative patterns aren't terribly problematic because they can so easily be corrected by making teachers aware of their impact and providing them with support they need to change course. Like the leaves of a tree, they are replaced over time.

In the final chapters of this book, we will discuss some of the challenges principals might face in supporting *all* teachers. We'll get going in Chapter 8 by discussing some common threats to teachers' purpose, priorities, and patterns—and what a principal can do to avoid them.

# 8

## Supporting a Range of Teacher Needs

*Mrs. B. loves her job as a high school chemistry teacher. She has a deeply rooted positive purpose and a good balance between her personal and professional priorities, and she is a role model of positive patterns. There is just one problem: as one of only a small handful of Black teachers on staff, she feels she is often looked upon to be the voice of Black students. Although she is happy to offer her perspective, as she would for any child of any race, she has begun to grow tired of her colleagues thinking she is a spokesperson for Black students.*

*The final straw came one spring day when she was actively teaching her class. Her students were deeply immersed in a chemistry lab. She was moving from group to group, answering questions, thrilled by their engagement and learning. Then her classroom phone rang: a Black student had been sent to the office for a common infraction. "He is upset," the principal said. "Can you come talk to him?"*

*The principal put Mrs. B. in a difficult position by asking her to leave her class to manage a situation about which she had no knowledge or prior input and for which she bore no responsibility. Should she go to the office and help navigate the situation? Should she leave the professional environment she was hired to work in to support a Black student just because she, too, is Black? Should she push back, pointing out that she was not in a position to intervene? Mrs. B. understood that the principal called her because he was uncertain himself. His own fears were motivating him to ask for help—but knowing this didn't help her feel any less uncomfortable. The call felt, to her, like a request to involuntarily shift her own purpose, priorities, and patterns.*

Teachers who belong to historically minoritized groups may face unique challenges in their professional journeys. In a 2016 article, author I. E. Smith does an excellent job of explaining the important distinction between the words *minority* and *minoritized*. The noun *minority*, Smith explains, simply means "a group of less than half of the total." By contrast, Smith writes, *minoritized* groups are those "that are different in race, religious creed, nation of origin, sexuality, and gender and as a result of social constructs have less power or representation compared to other members or groups in society."

These days, principals are hopefully doing a lot of studying, learning, and thinking about minoritized student groups, and they should do the same for minoritized teacher groups. Teachers of color, female teachers aspiring to leadership roles, LGBTQIA+ teachers, teachers with disabilities, teachers who are politically different from the local leanings—all these and more can feel unheard or marginalized by the greater community.

In Kate Rousmaniere's phenomenal 2013 book about the history of the principalship, *The Principal's Office*, she discusses the unintended consequences of the U.S. Supreme Court's 1954 *Brown v. Board of Education* decision in detail. Although Black educators had long been diminished in the profession, earning 60 percent less than their white counterparts, the desegregation order kicked off an entirely new sort of racism.

In the years that followed *Brown*, Black-only schools were often closed and students who had attended them were bused to previously white-only schools. Tens of thousands of Black educators were fired or demoted. By one estimate, in the South alone, 38,000 Black teachers lost their jobs. The number of Black principals was reduced by 90 percent. These drastic changes meant that one of the few professional positions available to educated African Americans was now far less open to them, and advocates and role models for Black children increasingly scarce. A full 50 years after the decision, only 14 percent of teachers were teachers of color (Lutz, 2017).

A dear friend of mine is a Black educator in a nearby district, and she remembers the day she told her parents she had decided to become a teacher. They discouraged her career choice. "Being a teacher was not a 'safe' career path, not in their eyes," she said. "They were worried I would be marginalized, moved around, transferred to difficult schools, viewed as the 'token Black.' They couldn't understand why I would want to be a teacher." She was determined, though—an indicator of positive purpose that is still present in her work—and has now spent two decades making inroads with students of all shapes, sizes, and colors.

I told this story to a colleague of mine who teaches in a part of the United States where there are many Black teachers. "Do you think considering a career as an educator is an 'unsafe' career path for Black college students?" I asked her.

"Not necessarily," she said, carefully considering the question. "Black teachers are out there. Look in the South. Look at the National Alliance of Black School Educators (NABSE). Look in urban districts. They're there, but they are not as often lifted into leadership roles or valued for their teaching skills as quickly or as readily as white educators are." Being a teacher of color in a profession dominated by white colleagues is a challenge that is not easily recognized or understood by white educators.

Other minoritized groups may shoulder similar isolating experiences. I'll never forget when I learned a reinforcing lesson about this. In a staff development meeting, I was working with a group on a list of commonly marginalized identities when a woman raised her hand. She had thus far been very quiet in the meeting, and when I called on her, she walked up to the front of the room—the first participant to do so—and clasped her hands nervously.

"We need to talk about age," she said. "There is a very distinct culture of ageism in education."

I saw other attendees sit up and listen as she explained. "We do it to our youngest teachers, by assuming they don't have the experience or wisdom needed to do this job well. We do it to our oldest teachers, by assuming they are too old, tired, and outdated to keep up. This is what I believe is happening to me. Because I am in the last few years of my career, I often feel isolated, as if I don't matter and don't have anything to contribute anymore. It's terribly insulting—and hurtful."

Several of her colleagues agreed, bravely standing up to share their own stories of ageism. "If teachers don't have a solid peer group within a school, they can be iced out from the group simply based on their age," one attendee summarized. "It's a terrible shame, because experienced teachers have enormous amounts of wisdom to contribute. But to contribute that wisdom, we have to be heard."

I was proud of the teachers who spoke. Perhaps we are all guilty of ageism in some form. Making assumptions about teachers who are either very young or reaching the end of their careers is unfair and misguided, and something we need to address rather than letting it define our schools.

The impact of minoritization is different for every individual. To empathize with minoritized teachers, the first thing those in the majority must understand is that we *can't* completely understand how they feel. What we *can* understand, simply by watching and listening, is the impact of minoritization on teachers' purpose, priorities, and patterns. They may feel lonely, disconnected, and hopeless, as though they aren't being seen or heard. They may find themselves questioning their place in the school community. In time, the school's culture might fray and reveal divides between staff.

# Acting Toward a Culture of Inclusion

Nothing good comes from teachers feeling like they don't belong. Either they will suffer alone, which will lead to negative patterns or priorities, or they will grow angry and bitter, which will threaten their purpose for teaching. Sometimes teachers choose to leave a particular school environment and teach somewhere their voice is valued and appreciated; other times, sadly, they may leave education altogether. What a loss this is for a school and the children it serves. Diversity of thought, experience, and background are necessary to create a school that welcomes all students and families. If we don't accept and embrace all teachers, how can we possibly accept and embrace all students? Here are some steps principals can take to ensure that they are promoting a culture of inclusion for everyone in their school.

## Acknowledging Your Own Microaggressions

Many principals have come to recognize that they, like all people, could be unintentionally transferring their implicit bias onto others. The risk of engaging in microaggressions is real, especially when we approach staff members with only our own experiences and schemas.

Arthur Forman, a well-known 19th century English cricketer who became a headmaster, addressed this risk when he said, "Not everyone thinks the way you think, knows the things you know, believes the things you believe, nor acts the way you would act. Remember this and you will go a long way in getting along with people." Recognizing our own tendencies to project our thinking, assumptions, and experiences on others is an important step in knowing how easily we could offend or hurt others.

A friend of mine once had her principal continuously call her the wrong name during an entire evaluation conference. The wrong name was close to her actual name, and some might have deemed it a small and inconsequential mistake, but to this teacher, it meant the principal hadn't truly invested in knowing her. To see her name repeatedly spelled wrong on a five-page evaluation document, and to hear it spoken wrong again and again, made her feel she was not seen or valued. In another example, I once had a difficult conversation with a colleague after she pointed out that I kept calling her "girl." I'd fallen into the habit of addressing any female friend or colleague that way—"Girl, you're the best!" or "You know what I mean, girl!" I'd intended it as a term of endearment for women I felt close to. My colleague pointed out that it was incredibly derogatory for women of color, dating back to times of slavery when enslavers would address an enslaved person as "boy" or "girl." I'd had no idea. Fortunately, my colleague understood my intentions and simply encouraged me to rethink my words. I did.

## Asking Questions

It is normal to feel anxious about doing or saying the wrong thing. We don't consciously want to offend or hurt others—but ironically, when this fear keeps us from learning more about others, it might cause us to unintentionally do exactly that. Teachers who experience constant minoritization would rather explain their experiences than feel marginalized, so principals should be open about asking questions to better understand those experiences.

I have found success in acknowledging that there are many things I do not know or understand. "I have limited knowledge about some of the struggles we are discussing today," I'll say. "What is it I might not understand about this situation?" Other questions might include "What am I missing here?" and "How might my schemas be out of place in this situation?" Asking questions with a genuine intent to know, learn, and do good things for teachers can be extremely enlightening and help promote inclusion.

# Addressing Issues of Exclusion

To address issues of exclusion in a school, here are six options principals might consider:

- **Look for it.** Some teachers keep to themselves because they are naturally introverted and prefer working alone, but others may do so because they don't feel part of the community—and it behooves a principal to be able to distinguish between the two. Again, simply asking questions is a great place to start: "Do you find your work lonely?" "Are there times you would rather be part of a team?" "Do you feel part of our school community?" "Is there anything I can do to help?"

- **See it.** If members of your staff are grouped by age, gender, political alignment, or race, this doesn't necessarily indicate a problem. I certainly enjoy spending time with colleagues of the same age and gender who are dealing with the same life and work issues that I am. However, if these groupings are pervasive, limiting, and divisive, then they may need to be addressed.

  If I suspect something like this is happening, I have an easy trick that helps. In a meeting or training, I will occasionally ask staff to split up and sit with colleagues with whom they don't usually interact. If certain staff members decline, or only reluctantly comply, that tells me they prefer not to open themselves up to others. Keeping an informal eye on ways they form social and professional groups will help you understand what motivates your teachers and how their actions affect your school.

- **Hear it.** Listening as teachers talk to—and about—one another is a skill that requires no extra time or energy—just the discipline to pay attention to the words being used. Do teachers speak professionally of one another, or does the school have a culture of gossip and put-downs? Do you hear events being planned to which certain staff members aren't invited? When you ask about inclusiveness, does silence or defensiveness serve as your answer? Ideally, a school will be blessed with the sounds of camaraderie, conversation, laughter, and shared stories among staff.

I once visited a school early on a Monday morning, in the half-hour before students arrived. It was sunny outside, and I had felt a little skip in my step at the onset of summer and the start of a new workweek. I was surprised, and then dismayed, to find the school's hallway silent and empty. All classroom doors were closed. "Um, where is everyone?" I asked the principal as he gave me a tour of the building. He shrugged. "Oh, they keep to themselves. I don't see them much this time of day." I was disappointed for him and for his staff. That before-school time can be a golden hour, a precious bit of time before students arrive for teachers to connect with one another both socially and professionally, to build collegiality and camaraderie and, ideally, a professional home.

- **Feel it.** Admittedly, the "feeling" of a school is impossible to quantify. It's especially hard when we are immersed in a school day after day. That's why I check in with substitutes, volunteers, or visitors to our school. I ask them how it felt to be part of our school community while there. Did they feel welcomed? Was there a sense of happiness in the building? Or was their experience one of cold, quiet, or standoffish interactions? Somewhere in between? Trying to capture an outsider's perception of the "feeling" of a building can tell a principal a lot about how staff feel on a regular basis.

- **Call it out.** Too many times, we sense something isn't right and we know we should act, but we don't. As principals, we don't have the luxury of assuming someone else should act against behavior that excludes others. It is our job to ensure that everyone has a voice. When seeing behaviors that may hurt or isolate others, a principal can say, "That's not how we do things here."

I once had a meeting with a subset of teachers who were angry at another group because they felt their workloads were unbalanced. When our conversation shifted toward personal comments directed at the second group, I knew I had to stop it immediately. "One of the things I love most about this school is that we don't say things like that—things that will divide or separate us as a unit," I said. "Let's work toward solutions, not divisions, and avoid critical judgment of our colleagues."

- **Eradicate it.** Principals are ultimately responsible for working to rid a school of exclusionary behaviors. A principal friend of mine was faced with this challenge when she had to address aggressive conversation-stealing from some members of her staff. In response, she instituted a conversation protocol with her teacher leadership team—a group of six teachers who were, perhaps unintentionally, conducting themselves in an exclusionary way during meetings. The principal instituted a rule that each person could speak for a set amount of time without interruptions from others. "We're going to commit to no interruptions. Period," she said, introducing the protocol with a smile—the "this is so serious we will joke about it" approach. After several months with this rule in place, she felt the point had been made; staff members were listening carefully when others spoke and weren't competing for their voices to be heard. Slowly, naturally, the "no interruptions" rule was relaxed and eventually abandoned. Whatever system you create to lessen the risk of isolation, it should ensure that each person on staff feels valued and accepted.

## Supporting Staff with Mental Health Needs

It is important for principals to understand that even the strongest, most purposeful teacher may have times of fragility and vulnerability. External and internal crises can lead to mental health challenges, even for those who have never dealt with such issues before. Professional expectations should never supersede mental health needs.

Different people have different pressure points at which they will falter. Many teachers are hard on themselves, battling self-criticism or insecurity. They might suffer from imposter syndrome, struggle to find meaning in their work, waffle between passion and apathy, or have trouble finding balance on the job. They might even know that their behaviors are unhealthy but feel unable to overcome them. Principals should do whatever they can to help teachers avoid reaching a breaking point. Professional lives aren't always full of joy, but they should never be places of despair, either.

Principals bear some responsibility for ensuring that their teachers work in an environment of inclusivity and acceptance, as this will help keep their purpose, priorities, and patterns on a positive path. In the next chapter, we'll discuss how principals can keep from feeling overwhelmed as they tackle this responsibility—and why the effort is worth the time it takes to do well.

# 9

## Fitting It All In

*Mr. M. is a relatively new principal. He knew the job would be complex and his to-do list long, which is proving to be true. He attends student events, oversees facility management, engages with parents, follows district and state mandates, and works with teachers to meet student needs. Many times, it seems he will never catch up. On top of all his responsibilities, he knows he should focus on supporting his staff, but he feels he has been neglecting them while other things take control of his days. He knows he needs some strategies to incorporate support for teachers into his other work.*

Principals can support teachers while fulfilling all their other responsibilities by recognizing teacher motivators, engaging in consistent oversight, and maintaining a positive outlook. By keeping teacher motivations on the front burner, principals can consistently see, value, and hear what teachers need. This isn't just one more thing among many; it is *the* thing. To ensure success, principals should assume good intentions on the part of staff. When we both assume good intentions and provide positive supports, we are released from any need to dominate or overpower struggling teachers. We work alongside them, not against them.

In working to build an inclusive and positive school culture, there are ways for principals to embed the monitoring of teacher purpose, priorities, and patterns into daily leadership practices. As with any investment, it is best to put time and resources in place up front, as the payoff will be more fruitful if we anticipate teacher needs rather than punish them for not meeting expectations. None of the suggestions in this chapter require adding anything extra to your plate; they can be implemented while you do what you would normally do as principal.

# Stacking

For principals with a large staff, the task of checking in with them daily or even weekly is impossible. This is where the concept of "stacking" comes in. The idea is to stack similar work together. So, for example, rather than doing one evaluation a day over five days, stack up five of them in one morning. Schedule an evening where you attend a music concert, PTO meeting, *and* a parent-teacher conference one right after another, talking with each teacher advisor immediately afterward so they know you were there in support of their activity. Sure, this can make for an exhausting day, but it forces you to focus on a particular part of your job in one go, thus freeing your mind—and your time—for other things later. When I mentor other principals, I explain that stacking can help them to better balance their personal and professional time.

I try to see every staff member every day, but on days when I'm overloaded with meetings and commitments, it's simply impossible. I make sure I'm checking in on a regular basis by clearing my calendar for a couple of hours two or three times a week to do so. Sometimes, when things are humming along and there are no big issues, my meandering walk through the building doesn't take long at all and I'm able to check in with everyone. Other times, I'll get caught up in a lengthy conversation with, say, the third teacher I encounter, and that's the end of my check-in. Regardless, each time, I walk away with a solid sense of how individuals on my staff are holding up. This way, they know that I care about them and that I will try to support them with any personal or professional challenges they may be facing.

## Being Available Versus Visible

For many years, successful principals strove to be thought of as "visible." Although I understand the value in teachers and students being able to see the principal frequently, this can have negative effects, too. If teachers feel "watched" or overly managed, the school culture can suffer.

If I'm spending all my time being seen, I might miss cues or clues about where I am actually needed. I prefer to be considered an "available" principal. I want teachers and students to know I am there when and if they need me, not when *I* decide they need me. I don't drop in or interrupt classes very often, but teachers know I am reachable by text, phone call, walkie-talkie call, or office check-in.

## Encouraging Teacher Self-Monitoring

When teachers recognize that their principal places value on purpose, understands the fluidity of priorities, and has specific expectations about patterns, it is easier to empower them to take ownership of their own motivational roots. They can reflect upon the status of their own careers, noting where they are in terms of purpose, priorities, and patterns, and identify areas they would like to improve.

This doesn't need to be a complicated or punitive process. Through trusting and honest conversations, a teacher can talk about all three issues without guilt or consequence. "I'm struggling right now" should not be a phrase a teacher is afraid to use with a principal. "Tell me more," a principal might say, guiding the teacher to consider whether the struggle is related to purpose, priorities, or patterns. The answer can lead to a coaching opportunity in which the principal and teacher come together to pull the teacher out of a rut and into a better professional place. When teachers can keep track of their own motivators and feel free to discuss them with the principal, the relationship grows stronger and more mutually beneficial.

# Using a Variety of Communication Tools

Nothing can replace one-on-one connection with another person. Slowing down to have a personal conversation is the best way for a principal to truly measure how a teacher is doing. Yet there are times when this simply can't happen. In those cases, an evening or weekend text or email can do the trick. Although I'll be the first to discourage principals from sending late-night emails with directives or work information, there is little harm in reaching out with good news, to let a teacher know you're thinking of them, or simply to check in.

Not long ago, a student in our building had a frightening seizure. The teacher did everything right—she cleared the room, called for medical help, secured backup from administrators, and comforted the child's mother as she climbed into the ambulance with her son. Afterward, I was called to handle another situation, and the nurse and teacher filled out the required forms to process the incident. That evening, I realized I'd never really checked back in on the teacher. Rather than call her and interrupt her night, I just sent a text to let her know I was thinking of her and was so proud of her. Then I asked, "How are you?"

"I'm OK," she wrote back. "I just wish I could have done more."

"There isn't a thing 'more' you could have done," I responded. "If that were my son, there's no one else on Earth I'd prefer to be watching over him at school."

She sent back a few hug emojis. Although I wish I could have talked to her in person, I went to sleep satisfied that I'd at least connected with her to see that she was OK. The next morning, I went to her room and had the one-on-one conversation I wanted to have. She was strong and positive, ready to take on a new day with the rest of her class, happy to have talked with the boy's mother and learned that he didn't seem to have a serious health condition. As I turned to leave, she said, "Thank you for your text. It meant a lot. It's nice to know you were thinking of me and wanted to be sure I was all right."

The exchange reinforced my belief that a quick compliment or message of support doesn't take a lot of time or planning—but it can go a long way.

## Setting Office Hours

Many principals tell their staff they have an open-door policy and encourage teachers to stop by anytime. Yet those same principals can feel conflicted when they find themselves working in their office too long, drawn by a desire to be out in the hallways and interacting with students. A friend of mind found a perfect solution to this quandary by setting office hours, both before and after school, during which she promises to be in her office. If something comes up and she can't be there, she simply puts a sign on the door indicating when she'll be back. She told me her office hours have become a revolving door of teachers coming by to say hello, give her a heads-up about any issues that might be brewing, or share information about their day. "I do everything I can to be there when I say I'll be there," she said, "and [teachers] have come to count on it. I can't always get to them, but they can always get to me."

## Refraining from Projecting Your Experiences on Others

I take great care not to project my own experiences on others, but it takes effort. It is, frankly, one of my biggest professional weaknesses. As an example, since I value organization and planning, I assume everyone should prioritize those two things. Since I have excellent attendance at work, I assume everyone else should. Because I cannot bring myself to leave a task undone, I think everyone else should finish their to-do list like I would. This kind of thinking isn't healthy, for me or for anyone else. It can be perceived as arrogant because it assumes that *my* way is the *best* way. But my way is *not* the best way, not by a long stretch, which is why I should never expect others to conduct themselves professionally as I would.

I became a better school leader when I accepted that my methods did not, could not, and should not apply to other people. I looked around at colleagues and staff members and realized they all had a slightly different version of purpose, priorities, and patterns—and all their systems seemed to be working quite well. Diversity in these areas is perfectly acceptable and even necessary. Poor leaders punish teachers who aren't like them. By contrast, strong leaders believe that we all benefit from a diverse staff of professionals. That isn't to say expectations shouldn't be set; it's just a reminder that expectations shouldn't be based on one principal's idea of perfection. Realizing this frees time for other priorities, because we don't have to waste time or energy trying to make everyone do things the way we would do them.

Accepting that teachers have varied professional approaches will help us embrace their differences rather than try to standardize them. The COVID-19 era helped many principals differentiate teacher needs, and that's a mindset we should pledge to keep for the future. Because the pandemic overruled our typical leadership decisions, we found we needed to err on the side of flexibility, recognizing that everyone had different degrees of fear about the virus, opinions on mitigation strategies, and comfort levels about when and how to return to school. Principals found that we needed to be tight on communication but loose about some of our previous expectations and standards. This experience helped us to allocate our time and energy where it belonged.

We are more efficient when we realize our leadership can flex with the needs of our teachers. We can recognize that what is a high priority for some might be a low priority for others. In the end, if students still have a positive experience, differences among educators should not be seen as problems that need fixing.

# Caring for Your Own Purpose

As the saying goes, you can't pour from an empty cup. Supporting diverse teachers means taking care of your own purpose, priorities, and patterns as well. Principals spend a lot of time making sure everyone in the school community is OK, and sometimes it can seem as though no one knows, appreciates, or even acknowledges the good work they do. This can be especially difficult if you were, in your teaching days, the type of teacher who had success in building relationships and making students flourish. If you were a purpose-driven teacher, it can feel especially lonely to spend most of your time propping others up to take on that role.

In Chapter 2, I told the story of a student who told me that I had been the only person to stick up for her when I was a teacher. After hearing her words, I found myself thinking a lot about teachers with positive purpose. My reflection was tinged with a bit of melancholy, because it is likely that few students would say such a thing about me now that I am a principal. Of course, I *do* stick up for kids, all day and every day, through my work with teachers and by committing to do what is best for kids. But the students don't necessarily know it.

This is how I see it: Though teachers can be intrinsically or extrinsically motivated, principals must be intrinsically motivated at all times. We stick up for teachers and students with every single decision we make, and no one may even realize it. But *we* do. If the task of taking care of others seems overwhelming, perhaps simply let it be so; don't chastise yourself for feeling occasional resentment or frustration. Being gentle with yourself—and your own motivational cycles—will help you be the best leader you can be.

Finding ways to focus on supporting all the teachers in your school—lifting them up when they are struggling and supporting them when they are meeting or exceeding expectations—is not a daunting task when it is embedded into your everyday work. One question we still need to address, though, is a simple but difficult one: How will you know that you're doing a good job? In the next chapter, we'll examine ways for principals to ensure that their efforts to support teachers are truly successful.

# How to Know Your Efforts
# Are Successful

*Ms. S. loves her job as a principal, and generally feels confident she is doing a good job connecting with her staff. Something nags at her, though. Even though she often asks teachers how they know their instruction has a positive impact on students, she recognizes that she isn't certain how to answer that question regarding her own work with teachers. How should she gather data and honest feedback? How can she be sure that information is valid and actionable? Measuring her own effectiveness in identifying and supporting teachers feels complicated and subjective, but she is certain it can be done. She wants to be intentional and thoughtful in the process. She begins to consider how she might survey her staff, capitalize on opportunities to gather helpful feedback, or use existing data to give her a true picture of her own effectiveness.*

It is difficult to measure the impact of a principal's efforts to identify and support teacher motivators. To know whether our approach is beneficial to teachers, it helps to seek targeted feedback from them and from applicable, measurable data that might already exist. In this chapter, we consider several practical and manageable ways, both formal and informal, for principals to gauge their progress and prowess in supporting teachers.

# Using Surveys and Data

School systems rely on data to drive and guide decision making, and principals can apply that same approach to evaluate their success in supporting teachers. Staff surveys—whether designed by the principal or supplied by a vendor—are a good way to collect and assess feedback from staff on your efforts.

## Self-Made Surveys

Some principals write their own questionnaires and send them out to staff. They ask for feedback on their leadership and collect suggestions for how to improve. A colleague of mine sends his teachers the same three questions at the beginning of every winter and summer break:

- What is going well for our school, staff, and students?
- What is not going well?
- What do you wish your principal would do differently?

The responses are anonymous, although the principal is often able to decipher which teacher authored which comments, especially when some of them consistently complain about the same issues. My colleague finds the responses helpful, particularly in identifying discontent or frustration. Many principals do something similar by creating and distributing their own surveys. Some use yes/no or multiple-choice questions, some use Likert scales, and some open answers up to short responses. The benefit to self-created surveys is that they are quick and free and provide immediate feedback.

## Research-Based Surveys

As easy and convenient as they may be, principal-made surveys are not standardized or necessarily based on best practices. It is difficult to be objective when asking others for feedback on our own work, so the questions we come up with may be flawed or too narrow and may not lead to diverse, balanced, or helpful responses. The questions may unintentionally ask multiple things at once, or they may lead respondents toward particular answers. Fortunately, there are several excellent survey tools on the market based on national benchmarks for responses from students, families, teachers, and staff. The companies that create these surveys administer them, provide in-depth reports, and help deconstruct analytics. They team up with school districts and principals to provide action steps in response to the survey answers. They can also help disaggregate responses by race, ethnicity, gender, socioeconomic status, and grade level. Since the principal isn't involved in the survey process beyond reading the responses, such surveys help ensure that questions are objective and responses can lead to improvements.

# Using Existing Data

In addition to surveys, principals can use school data as a form of teacher feedback. Here are a few ways to do so using information and systems that are already in place in most schools.

## Staff Attendance

Do your teachers tend to have solid attendance rates? When there are excessive absences, are you able to identify reasons why? I review a staff attendance report every nine weeks, and when there are teachers who have missed many days of school, I feel validated if I already know why—maternity or paternity leave, a family member who needed care, jury duty, or another unavoidable commitment. I am concerned when I see there are staff members who have missed a lot of days and I haven't offered support. I am also concerned if I see negative patterns emerging, such as a teacher calling off work every Friday or exploiting contractual loopholes to miss more school.

A principal I know in a nearby district struggles with teachers who take advantage of a liberal sick-leave policy. Too often, even minor appointments—a teacher's child's orthodontist check-in, picking up a new pair of contacts—turn into full-day absences. The principal feels his teachers don't even attempt to schedule these appointments before school, after school, or on breaks. "Maybe they don't think I understand the challenges of scheduling appointments," he told me, "but I don't think they recognize the impact on students when a teacher misses an entire day for a 15-minute appointment."

To remedy the situation, this principal is making himself, his assistant, and several support staff available to cover classes if a teacher needs to be slightly late to work to take care of these small appointments. "If I am willing to step in and help out, they can take care of personal priorities while also honoring their professional priorities," he theorizes.

## Engagement with Professional Development

I am a firm believer in letting staff choose professional development topics, and I try never to "force" teachers to attend a learning session they feel does not apply to them. But if we plan PD that speaks to a teacher's purpose, respects priorities, and helps reinforce positive patterns, teachers will be more likely to enjoy—and attend—PD sessions.

I consider staff PD attendance an indicator of my success as a leader. I am thrilled when all teachers attend our monthly PD sessions, and even more thrilled when I see them actively engaged in learning something new. It tells me that they recognize my attempts to honor their time and respect their needs, and they benefit by learning something new and becoming invested in instructional initiatives.

## Staff Meeting Exit Tickets

There is a popular meme that laments, "When the staff meeting could have been an email." My goal is to never have a staff meeting that could just as easily have been an email. I know it's inevitable that some teachers with a negative outlook will always feel any meeting is a waste. But if the large majority of teachers values our meetings, I take that as positive feedback.

So, how can we know if teachers find meetings worthwhile? I like to gather feedback by using staff meeting exit tickets that ask teachers questions like these:

- Do you feel today's meeting was worthwhile?
- Could today's meeting have been an email?
- Did we honor your time today?
- Will something in your instructional practice change as a result of today's meeting?
- Did you learn something new, or was the content presented today a repeat of information you already knew?

Responses will vary, but if most teachers answer that their time was well spent, I know that they appreciate the process.

## Parent Feedback

If parents are generally silent, we can always assume that no news is good news—or we can dig deeper and casually ask them about their experiences with their children's teachers. I've done this in the carpool line as I greet parents before and after parent-teacher conferences. "How are things going for your child?" I'll ask. "Do you feel your child's teachers have a good handle on her needs? Does she feel supported and challenged at school?" These casual conversations help me get a good qualitative view of the parent perspective.

Another option, one that provides quantitative data, is to keep a spreadsheet. List each teacher's name and enter an $X$ every time you hear something about a teacher. You can keep track of positive feedback in one column and negative feedback in another. Hopefully there will be very little negative feedback, but if you do receive any, it is worth digging for more specific information about what may have led to the discontent.

In his 2004 book *Class and Schools*, Richard Rothstein explains that the volume and intensity of parent input and feedback varies significantly by school, community, and situation. In some cases, parents feel "it is not [their] place to question how teachers perform their assigned tasks" (p. 32) because they consider education as an area outside their expertise and trust teachers to meet the requirements of their job classifications. In other words, they expect and trust teachers to do what they are hired to do. I have worked in schools where parents would never consider complaining about a teacher. By contrast, I have also worked in schools where parents were, in Rothstein's words, "so intrusive that it was impossible to deliver a coherent curriculum" (p. 32). It's a tricky balance for principals to encourage feedback from reluctant parents while also curtailing feedback from overbearing ones. The key is to recognize the difference and weigh the feedback accordingly. We can look for patterns and trends while taking care not to overreact or underreact to individual feedback. If multiple parents express concern about the same teacher, reviewing a teacher's purpose, priorities, or patterns to see if there is a justification for the complaints is warranted.

## The Evaluation Process

Every time principals evaluate a teacher, they are succumbing to the teacher's evaluation of them, too. Teachers can gauge how they are treated, whether their voices are valued, and whether the principal cares to know them as individuals. Principals who make evaluations one-sided, taking an aggressive or domineering approach, are eliminating one of the most powerful feedback tools they have.

A friend of mine who works in Human Resources told me about a disciplinary hearing he'd had for a principal in his district. "The principal actually *boasted* that he liked to push his teachers so hard to improve and 'be better' that teachers often left evaluation conferences in tears," my friend said. "I had to point out that teachers leaving in tears is *not* a sign of a strong leader—it is the sign of a weak leader."

Far from dreading their evaluation conferences, teachers should look forward to them as chances to officially collaborate to review successes and address weaknesses. For principals, discussing how teachers are implementing their purpose, balancing their priorities, and maintaining positive patterns is a huge benefit of the formal evaluation process, because typically the conferences create an environment to discuss each of these components at length. There is also time to ask for and receive feedback. "It's important to me that you feel I understand your purpose, your priorities, and your patterns," a principal might say. "Let's talk about how each of these components affects your work and whether you think I have a grasp on each. If I don't, let's talk about how I can do better." Reciprocal feedback will make these meetings beneficial for both parties.

Many principals also engage in shorter informal evaluation opportunities throughout the year in the form of walkthroughs or instructional rounds, during which they might observe a classroom and then share brief feedback with the teacher. Informal evaluations also occur during debriefings after parent-teacher meetings, hallway conversations, and teacher visits to the principal's office. If you've spoken with each teacher and learned a little bit more about what makes them tick, whether in a formal or in an informal setting, that's a sign you are successfully responding to their needs.

## Reading the Room

Not long ago, I talked with a teacher whose patterns seemed to be a little off. During her evaluation conference, I made note of a few things I hoped she'd work toward improving. I was talking fast, offering suggestions without pausing to consider how she was responding. Her face was blank, and I assumed she was just taking it all in. When our meeting was over, I said, "Is there anything you'd like me to know?"

She told me she had nothing to add.

"Are you sure?" I asked.

She nodded, signed her evaluation, and left the room quietly. I felt unsettled and uncertain. After school, I went to see her again.

"I don't feel right about our meeting," I told her.

Her face softened. "I don't, either," she said, sinking down to her chair.

"You go first," I said, sitting across from her.

"I didn't feel like I had a chance to explain myself," she began. As she spoke, I realized I'd assumed her lapse in patterns just indicated a lack of self-discipline or planning routines. In fact, she told me, she had just begun a round of in vitro fertilization treatments and was feeling sick, miserable, and depressed. Her patterns weren't the problem; her priorities had shifted to starting a family.

I felt terrible for letting my assumptions get in the way of seeing her situation clearly. I also felt terrible for not checking in with her more often as she and her partner took on this difficult challenge. We spoke for a long time, and in the end, she assured me she would keep me posted about anything that might affect her work. She also promised to let me know if there was anything I could do to help. Just 12 months later, she welcomed a baby girl into the world. This experience was a good reminder to me to always look for signs and signals teachers send that reveal their purpose, priorities, and patterns.

## Analyzing How You Respond to Feedback

I find it is much easier to respond to feedback than to analyze *how* I respond to feedback. It's easy enough for principals to absorb feedback and quickly "fix" things that are wrong. If teachers complain about the schedule, for instance, a principal can usually make some staffing shifts and solve the problem. If parents say the bus dismissal area is crowded, the principal can start to think about ways to make it safer. No problem.

It's much harder to stop and think about *how* you typically respond when you get feedback. If there is a consistent pattern to your responses, you might be able to glean how others perceive you. I am not proud to admit that I usually feel defensive when I initially hear feedback. I have learned to recognize the signs: my face feels flushed and I experience a complex mix of resentment, anger, and frustration. An internal voice protests, "Wait, wait, wait. That's not right. There's more to the story."

I have worked very hard to avoid this initial reaction, and with time, I have learned to overcome the reaction when it happens. I can recognize the defensiveness, acknowledge it, and move on to the productive part—the part where I absorb and accept the feedback as reflecting people's truth about their experiences with my leadership.

"I don't really receive much feedback, even when I ask for it," a principal once told me. I encouraged him to monitor how others perceived his reaction to feedback. "If your staff won't tell you, ask some trusted friends or colleagues," I said. "Ask your spouse. Ask your kids. See what they say."

He emailed me months later. "Well, you were right. I asked my wife, and her answer wasn't easy for me to hear," he admitted. "She told me I always appear annoyed when people try to give me constructive criticism. Apparently, I seem too busy or too distracted to listen, and I quickly move on to other topics before I work through the issue. My wife told me she suspects my teachers sense my annoyance and have just given up on giving me feedback."

Here are some questions to ask yourself or someone you trust about the way you respond to feedback:

- What is my body language like?
- Is my reaction alienating to others?
- Do I ignore feedback I don't like?
- If I disagree with the feedback, do I still try to respond?
- Does feedback make me feel I've failed?
- Do people continue to give feedback when I ask for it?

## Asking Your Harshest Critics

It can be helpful to ask for feedback from teachers you know are highly critical of you. This takes courage, but it can offer insight into your blind spots and may shift your leadership style in positive ways. And as a bonus, doing this can help dissipate conflict between you and the teacher.

I once worked with a teacher who often found fault with my leadership decisions. Her criticism affected her colleagues, who were torn between trying to defend me and showing a collegial solidarity with her.

One day, in a burst of courage, I asked this teacher to have lunch with me. Reluctantly, she agreed. I ordered sandwiches to be delivered to school. We sat down to discuss what she thought was going well at our school, what she thought was problematic, and what she wished I would do differently to help teachers. Although I am sure she softened her harshest critiques, I was pleased when she opened up with her frustrations. She was able to see my point of view, and I was able to see how she perceived some of my decisions, giving me the chance to absorb her critiques.

It took a lot of courage for me to meet with the teacher—I distinctly remember taking many deep breaths while walking to her room, sandwiches in hand—but I was glad I'd done it. As a result of our conversation, I made some tweaks to my leadership patterns, and she seemed to offer me a bit more grace.

## Seeking Out an Accountability Partner

It helps for principals to have an accountability partner— someone who understands how they think and work—to point out their blind spots. A few years ago, I was lucky enough to have an assistant principal, Jaclyn, who was an excellent partner in accountability. We pushed one another forward professionally, each nudging the other when there was something we weren't seeing or doing right. She was an eager and skilled leader who provided feedback and guidance when I needed it, just as I did for her; together, we developed a rhythm of reciprocal feedback. I could ask her, "Am I being too hard on this teacher?" or "Is this something we should just let go?" She would answer honestly. "You have a soft spot for that teacher," she said once, "so you're not seeing troublesome patterns. They should be addressed before they cause a rift in our staff." Another time, she cautioned, "You like to give teachers a break. But that teacher's lack of purpose is causing problems in the classroom. Take a look. I think it's something we need to address."

Jaclyn has since moved on to lead her own school, and I miss her in-house professional support, but I still call her for accountability conversations. I have a few other colleagues, too, who can elbow me back into shape when needed. This can take any shape or form, depending on who you have in your network and who you trust to hold you accountable. Earlier I mentioned a principal who received honest feedback from his wife. Although she was not a professional colleague, she knew her husband well enough, and felt safe enough, to tell him the truth. Having someone trustworthy around who is happy to push you to improve yourself will ultimately make you a better leader.

## Watching Yourself

"When the principal has a cold, the entire school has a cold." Those were the wise words of one of my supervisors, years ago, describing how a principal's actions and behaviors reverberate among staff and students. She was being quippy, but her words rang true. If the principal is overwhelmed and frantic, staff will be overwhelmed and frantic. If the principal feels lonely and isolated, so, too, will staff. If you feel unsettled at work, it is likely your staff does, too. Are you anxious? Do you have empathy fatigue? Are you tired or stressed? It's worth considering how you, as principal, feel, because it's likely that those feelings have rubbed off on others. Put another way, how you respond to professional challenges may reflect how your teachers respond as well.

## Absorbing the Good

Sometimes it is difficult for principals to accept positive feedback, especially when they come from staff members who benefit from having us in their corner. When I was a teacher, I once told my principal I appreciated her hard work organizing a diversity event for our community. She acted as if she hadn't heard me, bustling down the hall without acknowledging my compliment. I followed her, intent on thanking her.

"Listen. Really, that was great," I told her.

"Sure. Yes," she replied. "What can I do for you?"

"Nothing," I said, my voice betraying my confusion. "I was just giving you a compliment."

"Sorry." She stopped, looked at me, and exhaled. "I'm just not used to positivity without strings." Her distrust made me feel sad for her, but now that I am a principal, I recognize how she felt. When staff members thank me or tell me they appreciate my efforts, I assume they say it because they feel they must, or because they need something else from me, or maybe just because they have good manners. Being a principal convinces us that most of what we do will not be appreciated and is always up for criticism. But we should be cautious about disregarding positive feedback. In fact, we *should* accept it—and absorb its meaning. No one is perfect, but we can come pretty darn close, skillfully supporting our teachers through a very complicated and exhausting career. Every now and then, we should pause, reflect, and recognize that our efforts have paid off. And take a compliment.

If teachers know they are supported, if they know their principal will not overreact to small missteps, if there is consistent compassion and empathy, if expectations are clear and fair, if teachers don't fear for their jobs because of the challenges they face in their lives—if all these conditions are in place, teachers will be happy to offer principals feedback. If the opposite is true, they may be more reluctant to share their perspectives unless given the opportunity to offer critical feedback without fear of retribution. Regardless, it's worth the effort to really find out how teachers feel about your support. Doing so will enhance the strength of their purpose, help them to balance their priorities, and have a positive impact on their daily patterns.

# Conclusion

As we've discussed throughout this book, teachers face any number of personal and professional challenges over the course of their careers. Personal obstacles are just that—personal—and thus there is very little a principal can or should do to control or manage them. But personal and professional lives often overlap, and both can impact a teacher's effectiveness.

How teachers approach their work is usually influenced by multiple factors. A teacher might have a positive purpose but negative priorities that lead to negative patterns. Or a teacher may exhibit positive patterns and priorities, but a negative purpose. Motivators bleed together and shift, back and forth and back again, as time passes. Understanding motivation is not an exact science. The process of identifying and considering what drives professional actions is fluid. With that said, identifying teacher motivators can help us to understand why a teacher may be succeeding or struggling—and, hopefully, this book provides a roadmap for responding accordingly.

Principals' legacies are determined by how they treat, value, and support their staff. Teachers want a supervisor who sees them, who understands the challenges they face in their lives, who sets high expectations but is eager to offer a break when needed. If this is how we want to be seen, and we understand that our other responsibilities become less stressful when our teachers feel empowered, helping them becomes a simple, manageable, and even enjoyable task. We just need to continue to ask ourselves how purpose, priorities, and patterns contribute to teachers' current work.

As we conclude this book, there are two final thoughts I'd like you to take with you. The first centers on having hard conversations. Talking with teachers about problems in their professional practice can be daunting, but it's possible to say very hard things with a soft touch. Occasionally, this can be misinterpreted as being *too* soft. Finding a balance between accountability and leniency allows principals to be seen as leaders who will set expectations and help teachers meet them, but who are quick to intervene when they don't.

A principal colleague of mine once received feedback on his evaluation indicating he didn't have "hard conversations."

"I think you avoid saying difficult things to teachers," his supervisor said. "I worry you are seen as a pushover."

"Why would you think I'm a pushover?" My friend was almost speechless.

"Well," his supervisor said, "you get zero complaints from the union, so I figured you were avoiding complicated issues. Do you let things go too often? Do you avoid hard conversations?"

My friend, still shocked and dismayed, finally found the words to explain that the opposite was true. "I have hard conversations all the time. But I handle them with grace and compassion, which is why you're not hearing complaints." He talked about multiple occasions that year when he'd met with teachers to outline suggested improvements, and showed plenty of evidence that he'd carefully and thoughtfully monitored those improvements. His supervisor appreciated his explanations and rewrote his evaluation to read as follows: "The principal is empathetic and compassionate, leading staff through complicated issues without upsetting them or making them feel devalued. He is strong but does not attempt to lead by intimidation. He is forceful, but not overly so."

Although it is unfortunate that the supervisor had initially assumed the worst, the principal had actually created an ideal leadership balance: he'd led his staff toward high expectations without negatively affecting the school culture, without hurting feelings, without causing anger or defensiveness. The lack of complaints from his staff wasn't because he was reluctant to be the "bad guy"; it was the result of a leader who targeted intentional, honest, gentle feedback to the people who needed it.

Finally, I'd like to take a moment to reinforce the value of understanding and compassion when working with teachers. After all, it's unfair for principals to insist they want teachers to be patient and kind to students if they themselves don't treat teachers this way. When a teacher stumbles and needs help, the principal should rely on grace and forgiveness rather than frustration.

I learned this lesson firsthand early in my teaching career. After three years of teaching, I felt I had established myself as someone who was dependable and dedicated. Then I had a *really* bad month. It started randomly: I was teaching one day and was struck by the absolute certainty that I'd left my oven on with a breakfast sandwich inside. Frantic, I told my assistant principal, Mr. B., that I had to go home before my apartment burned down. He covered my class. Later that week, I lost my keys at home and had to arrive at work an hour late. The next week, my washer broke and water flooded my bathroom and bedroom, requiring me to spend an entire day waiting for a technician to come fix the washer. By the end of that day, I had a migraine—the only one of my life—and spent the next three days sicker than I've ever been. I went back to school too soon, tried to make it through the day, and vomited in a mad dash to the restroom. A few days later, finally recovered, I had to miss another day to attend a memorial service.

I was embarrassed and mortified at the amount of school I'd missed, especially knowing my colleagues and assistant principal had to scramble to cover my classes. I went into Mr. B.'s office to apologize. He smiled kindly. "Life happens," he said. "Let's just hope your bad-luck streak ends soon." Seeing my face, he reassured me even further. "But if it doesn't, don't worry; we will figure it out. Everyone goes through times when we feel stretched thin. Don't be hard on yourself. I've never doubted your commitment, and I appreciate everything you do for our school."

Mr. B.'s words were like an elixir to my anxiety. His kindness and patience that day were indicative of his approach to students and staff alike and made me even more loyal and dedicated—to the school, certainly, but also to him, an administrator who saw and heard my concern and reassured me that he still valued and trusted me.

Teachers deserve to work in a school environment where they are held to high standards. When they come to their jobs with a positive purpose, they are committed to providing an excellent learning experience for their students. When their priorities are balanced and positive, they provide dedication and focus for their students. And when they exhibit positive patterns, they display the behaviors we expect from well-prepared expert teachers. If a principal understands all the ways to support a teacher's motivators, students, staff, and the school community will all flourish together.

# References

*Brown v. Board of Education*, 347 U.S. 483 (1954).

Davis, J., & Wilson, S. M. (2000). Principals' efforts to empower teachers: Effects on teacher motivation and job satisfaction and stress. *The Clearing House, 73*(6), 349–353. https://doi.org/10.1080/0009865 0009599442

Dinham, S., & Scott, C. (1996, April). *Teacher satisfaction, motivation and health: Phase one of the Teacher 2000 Project.* Paper presented at a meeting of the American Educational Research Association, New York. (ERIC Document Reproduction Service No. ED 405 295)

Douglas, S. C., & Martinko, M. J. (2001). Exploring the role of individual differences in the prediction of workplace aggression. *Journal of Applied Psychology, 86*(4), 547.

Jackson, P. N. (1968). *Life in classrooms.* Holt, Rinehart and Winston.

Lutz, M. (2017). The hidden cost of *Brown v. Board:* African American educators' resistance to desegregating schools. *Online Journal of Rural Research & Policy, 12*(4). https://newprairiepress.org/ojrrp/vol12 /iss4/2/

Packer, J. L. (2016). *Teacher perception of feedback through the Ohio Teacher Evaluation System and the effect on teacher efficacy* [Unpublished doctoral dissertation]. The Ohio State University.

Rothstein, R. (2004). *Class and schools: Using social, economic, and educational reform to close the black-white achievement gap.* Teachers College Press.

Rousmaniere, K. (2013). *The principal's office: A social history of the American school principal.* SUNY Press.

Sehgal, P., Nambudiri, R., & Mishra, S. K. (2017). Teacher effectiveness through self-efficacy, collaboration and principal leadership. *International Journal of Educational Management, 31*(4), 505–517. https://doi.org/10.1108/ijem-05-2016-0090

Short, P. M., & Rinehart, J. S. (1992, April). *Teacher empowerment and school climate.* Paper presented at a meeting of the American Educational Research Association, San Francisco. (ERIC Document Reproduction Service No. ED 347 678)

Sinclair, C. (2008). Initial and changing student teacher motivation and commitment to teaching. *Asia-Pacific Journal of Teacher Education, 36*(2), 79–104.

Smith, I. E. (2016, September 2). Minority vs. minoritized: Why the noun just doesn't cut it. *The Odyssey Online.* www.theodysseyonline.com/minority-vs-minoritize

Wahlstrom, K. L., & Louis, K. S. (2008, October 1). How teachers experience principal leadership: The roles of professional community, trust, efficacy, and shared responsibility. *Educational Administration Quarterly, 44*(4), 455–495.

Watson, D., & Clark, L. A. (1984). Negative affectivity: The disposition to experience aversive emotional states. *Psychological Bulletin, 96*(3), 465.

# Index

# About the Author

**Jen Schwanke** has been an educator for 24 years, teaching or leading at all levels. She is the author of two previous books: *You're the Principal! Now What? Strategies and Solutions for New School Leaders* and *The Principal Reboot: 8 Ways to Revitalize Your School Leadership*. She has also written for *Choice Literacy, Education Week Teacher, Principal*, and *Principal Navigator*. She is a frequent cohost and contributor to *Principal Matters: The School Leader's Podcast*. She presents at conferences for ASCD, NAESP, Battelle for Kids, RRCNA, and various state and local education organizations. She has provided professional development to various districts in the areas of school climate, personnel, and instructional leadership. She is an instructor in educational administration at Miami University. Having worked as a principal for 17 years, she is currently serving as a deputy superintendent in Dublin, Ohio. More information can be found on her website, www.jenschwanke.com.

# Related ASCD Resources: School Leadership

At the time of publication, the following resources were available (ASCD stock numbers appear in parentheses).

**Print Products**

*The Aspiring Principal 50: Critical Questions for New and Future School Leaders* by Baruti K. Kafele (#120023)

*The Assistant Principal 50: Critical Questions for Meaningful Leadership and Professional Growth* by Baruti K. Kafele (#121018)

*The Coach Approach to School Leadership: Leading Teachers to Higher Levels of Effectiveness* by Jessica Johnson, Shira Leibowitz, and Kathy Perret (#117025)

*Committing to the Culture: How Leaders Can Create and Sustain Positive Schools* by Steve Gruenert and Todd Whitaker (#119007)

*Compassionate Coaching: How to Help Educators Navigate Barriers to Professional Growth* by Kathy Perret and Kenny McKee (#121017)

*Leadership for Learning: How to Bring Out the Best in Every Teacher, 2nd Edition* by Carl Glickman and Rebecca West Burns (#121007)

*Navigating the Principalship: Key Insights for New and Aspiring School Leaders* by James P. Spillane and Rebecca Lowenhaupt (#118017)

*The Principal as Chief Empathy Officer: Creating a Culture Where Everyone Grows* by Thomas R. Hoerr (#122030)

*The Principal Reboot: 8 Ways to Revitalize Your School Leadership* by Jen Schwanke (#121005)

*Qualities of Effective Principals, 2nd Edition* by James H. Stronge and Xianxuan Xu (#121022)

*Stop Leading, Start Building: Turn Your School into a Success Story with the People and Resources You Already Have* by Robyn R. Jackson (#121025)

*What If I'm Wrong? And Other Key Questions for Decisive School Leadership* by Simon Rodberg (#121009)

*What's Your Leadership Story? A School Leader's Guide to Aligning How You Lead with Who You Are* by Gretchen Oltman and Vicki Bautista (#121020)

*You're the Principal! Now What? Strategies and Solutions for New School Leaders* by Jen Schwanke (#117003)

For up-to-date information about ASCD resources, go to **www.ascd.org**. You can search the complete archives of *Educational Leadership* at **www.ascd.org/el**.

**ASCD myTeachSource®**

Download resources from a professional learning platform with hundreds of research-based best practices and tools for your classroom at http://myteachsource.ascd.org/.

For more information, send an email to member@ascd.org; call 1-800-933-2723 or 703-578-9600; send a fax to 703-575-5400; or write to Information Services, ASCD, 2800 Shirlington Road, Suite 1001, Arlington, VA 22206 USA.